C000150148

CREATION:
CHANCE OR DESIGN?

CREATION:
CHANCE OR DESIGN?

David J. Tyler

EVANGELICAL PRESS

EVANGELICAL PRESS
Faverdale North Industrial Estate, Darlington, DL3 0PH,
England

Evangelical Press USA
P. O. Box 825, Webster, New York 14580, USA

e-mail: sales@evangelicalpress.org
web: www.evangelicalpress.org

© Evangelical Press 2003. All rights reserved. No part of
this publication may be reproduced, stored in a retrieval
system or transmitted, in any form, or by any means,
electronic, mechanical, photocopying, recording or otherwise, without the prior permission of the publishers.

First published 2003

British Library Cataloguing in Publication Data available

ISBN 0 85234 544 5

Unless otherwise indicated, Scripture quotations in this
publication are from the Holy Bible, New International
Version. Copyright © 1973, 1978, 1984, International Bible
Society. Used by permission of Hodder & Stoughton, a
member of the Hodder Headline Group. All rights
reserved.

Printed and bound in Great Britain by Creative Print and
Design Wales, Ebbw Vale, South Wales.

To Sheena

ACKNOWLEDGEMENTS

I am grateful to John Peet, Paul Garner and Sylvia Baker and other members of the Biblical Creation Society for numerous discussions over the past twenty years, all of which have helped to develop my own thinking. Several friends have provided critical and constructive feedback on earlier drafts of this guide. Sheena, my wife, has given me extensive feedback on the whole manuscript and the final result is much improved as a result of her comments. Philip Snow provided most of the illustrations and I am grateful for the way he has translated my ideas for artwork. My thanks to Sheena Tyler who created the cartoon in chapter 11. Sources of other illustrations are acknowledged in the text.

CONTENTS

INTRODUCTION

In the year 2002, creation became national headlines in Britain for at least two weeks. The underlying issue appeared to be faith schools, which many political activists dislike intensely. However, to attack Anglican and Roman Catholic schools would have been to alienate many voters with Anglican or Roman Catholic allegiances. To attack Islamic schools would have been deemed racist. So when Emmanuel College in Gateshead, England, which openly declares its Christian ethos, opened its doors to a Saturday Creation Conference, the opponents of faith schools were quick to launch an attack.

The 'creation' word was deemed so evidently wrong that even debating the issues could not be allowed. Evaluation of evidences was not on the agenda. School inspectors had recently approved the work of the college and this greatly inconvenienced the objectors. The critics wanted the college re-inspected — implying that the job had not been done properly. Also inconvenient was the way pupils and parents generally praised the college, and finding anyone who objected to its Christian stance was difficult. Nevertheless, the fuming and the outrage continued because, they said, it is unthinkable that creationism could be allowed any place in education!

Noticeably lacking in the national media was any exploration of the issues. Few pointed out that most of the speakers at the conference had degrees in science, and one was a professor at a British university. Also lacking was any real understanding of why Christians wanted to challenge evolutionary theories of origins on both biblical and scientific grounds. Most rarely got beyond mutterings about 'fundamentalism'. But one good point did get publicity. The college was not seeking to exclude evolutionary theories from its educational process, but to help students critically evaluate such theories and consider alternative explanations of the evidence. The emphasis was on opening up the issues, not brainwashing young people with one set of standard answers.

This is the basic approach that I have adopted for this guide. My concern is to open up the subject of origins and to make it accessible to a new generation of Christians. I have focused on the biblical teaching on creation, and have pointed out how the Bible can inform our thinking on a host of related subjects. My concern is with foundational principles rather than details.

This guide sets out to help readers:

• Ask the right questions (rather than supplying ready-made answers)

- Distinguish between what is known from the Bible and what should be determined by science
- Focus on the central issues (the chapters identify relevant areas where the Bible speaks about origins, but does not elaborate on technical matters)
- Recognize that biblical Christianity can coexist harmoniously with science.

The Guide sets out to address central issues. The book is written with the conviction that the biblical teaching on origins is foundational to the gospel and to the Christian mindset. However, I am well aware that some contemporary Christians deem this whole issue secondary. About forty years of grappling with origins questions has confirmed repeatedly to me that they are making a serious mistake. Not only are the issues central for developing a Christian mind, they are foundational to the gospel message itself. It is my prayer that these chapters will both stimulate thought and contribute to a new consensus emerging from within the Christian community.

The Guide seeks to engage with contemporary culture about the meaning and relevance of truth. This is actually a very significant issue for Christians. Ignoring it means that our witness to the Lord Jesus Christ is impoverished and we may end up talking only to ourselves. There are three widely held solutions to the question 'What is truth?'

a. The *science* solution — the only route to truth is through science. Leaders of many organizations claiming to promote science appear to believe that the only way to practise science is to say that God should have no place in our thinking. They claim that 'Nature is all there is.' Their philosophical position is called naturalism, and they say that this alone is the route to knowing anything worthwhile.

b. The *post-modern* solution — this answer insists that truth is always relative and subjective, never absolute and objective. This position is not strong in scientific circles, but it is very widespread elsewhere. Almost everyone holding to any absolute truth is termed a 'fundamentalist' by this group.

c. The *Christian* solution. Jesus says, 'I am the way, the truth and the life' (John 14:6). He reveals 'true truth' to us. Here is knowledge that comes to us, not by man seeking it out but by God making it known. This revealed truth is vital for us to live in the real world (rather than one of our own imagination).

Beliefs about origins are fundamental to most belief systems and they are at the heart of the Christian gospel. They deal with basic questions such as 'Who is God and what is he like?'; 'What is Man?'; 'What is sin?'; 'Is death normal?' — and if it is, 'Why do we feel grief and pain when we encounter death?'

The Guide is intended as a stimulus to understanding biblical teaching. We shall be looking at what science is and how it relates to revelation. We shall be thinking about ways in which Genesis impacts on scientific work. The last three chapters discuss specific evidences relating to origins. However, there are innumerable technical issues that we shall not consider — for example, assessing the Big Bang theory and interpreting geologic data. It is not that these are unimportant issues, but our priority here is to work through the foundations. Without a good grounding in what God has revealed, interest in technical issues can do little more than satisfy intellectual curiosity.

HOW TO USE *THE GUIDE*

Creation: chance or design? is the latest book in a new series called *The Guide*. This series will cover books of the Bible on an individual basis, such as *Colossians and Philemon*, and relevant topics such as *Christian comfort,* and this work on creation. The aim of the series is to communicate the Christian faith in a straight-forward and readable way.

Each book in *The Guide* will cover a book of the Bible or topic in some detail, but will be contained in relatively short and concise chapters. There will be questions at the end of each chapter for personal study or group discussion, to help you to study the Word of God more deeply.

An innovative and exciting feature of *The Guide* is that it is linked to its own web site. As well as being encouraged to search God's Word for yourself, you are invited to ask questions related to the book on the web site, where you will not only be able to have your own questions answered, but also be able to see a selection of answers that have been given to other readers. The web site can be found at www.evangelicalpress.org/TheGuide. Once you are on the site you just need to click on the 'select' button at the top of the page, according to the book on which you wish to post a question. Your question will then be answered either by Michael Bentley, the web site co-ordinator and author of *Colossians and Philemon*, or others who have been selected because of their experience, their understanding of the Word of God and their dedication to working for the glory of the Lord.

Other books already published in the series include *The Bible book by book, Ecclesiastes, Job, Esther* and, in the topical series, *Revolutionary forgiveness*; many more will follow. It is the publisher's hope that you will be stirred to think more deeply about the Christian faith, and will be helped and encouraged in living out your Christian life, through the study of God's Word, in the difficult and demanding days in which we live.

CHAPTER ONE

UNDERSTANDING GENESIS

LOOK IT UP

BIBLE READING

Acts 17:11

INTRODUCTION

Having two young sons has certainly been a lot of fun for me. They really enjoy being read to and are discovering that there are many different kinds of books. Sometimes we read about the natural world, or about farming, or about how water comes through our taps. They understand that these books are describing the world around us and explain how things work. Sometimes we read about Rupert Bear, or Peter Rabbit, or Percy the Park Keeper. They know that someone has made up these stories for fun. Such books entertain and stir the imagination.

There are other stories that are different again, such as a children's version of *The Pilgrim's Progress* by John Bunyan, or *The Lion, the Witch and the Wardrobe* by C. S. Lewis. It was not long before my sons were asking questions about what we were reading. They soon realized that some types of literature have a symbolism and deeper meaning.

The need to interpret the words of Scripture

Similarly, it should not take too long for even casual readers of the Bible to realize that it is made up of different types of literature. Some books are historical, recounting events in Israel's past or in the life of Jesus. Some books, like the Psalms, are poetic and written for public and private worship. Some, like Proverbs and Ecclesiastes, are written to impart wisdom. There are many books named after prophets that are sometimes historical, sometimes poetic and sometimes contain imagery and symbolism.

Most of the New Testament books are letters, full of teaching, advice, warnings and encouragements for the readers. It is very important to know what type of literature we are reading in the Bible, as this will affect the way we understand the words. We are going to look at three principles that will help us when we examine the Scriptures (Acts 17:11).

1. God speaks so that we can know what he is saying

Throughout the Bible, it is clear that God has things to say to us. When he gave the Law to the Israelites through Moses, he made it plain by the words he used and by the things he did at the time. When he spoke to the people through the prophets, the people heard words they understood — even though they generally did not welcome the content. When Jesus preached, people flocked to hear him — they understood what he taught and were amazed at his authority. So also was the apostolic preaching and teaching: Christianity is not a mystery religion! The message of the gospel is for ordinary people and not for a secret society or an elite! The messengers of Christ are called to speak plainly and simply. The Apostles could all say: 'in Christ we speak before God with sincerity, like men sent from God' (2 Corinthians 2:17; see also 4:2).

2. Our sinfulness affects the way we think

Although the Bible is written for ordinary people, and we do not have to have special training to understand what God is saying, it is a matter of history that the message of Scripture has been continually misunderstood. Sometimes, this is because we do not appreciate the context, or because a particular truth is not directly relevant to our present needs. However, the root problem is not that we live in a different culture, nor that we are dumb, nor that we are dependent on imperfect translators, but rather that we are sinful. We want the Scriptures to bring us a different message! The result is that we read God's Word through tinted glass that conceals the truths we do not like and somehow conveys the teachings we want to hear. Often this is done by choosing the teachers we want to hear and closing our ears to people who bring us a message we do not approve of. Both Old and New Testaments warn us about this. Jeremiah rebukes the people of his day with these words:

'How can you say, "We are wise,
    for we have the law of the LORD,"
when actually the lying pen of the scribes has
    handled it falsely?
The wise will be put to shame;
    they will be dismayed and trapped.
Since they have rejected the word of the LORD,
    what kind of wisdom do they have?'

                                (Jeremiah 8:8-9).

Here is a situation where the people felt comfortable, but they were actually in great danger. Their religious leaders were handling the Law of God in a false way, but the people did not care. They were being fed teachings they wanted to hear.

The same situation is apparent in the pages of the New Testament Scriptures. Paul writes:

For the time will come when men will not put up with sound doctrine. Instead, to suit their own desires, they will gather around them a great number of teachers to say what their itching ears want to hear. They will turn their ears away from the truth and turn aside to myths

                                (2 Timothy 4:3-4).

In opposition to this, Paul directs his readers, in the first instance, back to Scripture: 'All Scripture is God-breathed and is useful for teaching, rebuking, correcting and training in righteousness, so that the man of God may be thoroughly equipped for every good work' (2 Timothy 3:16).

So, our first need is to understand Scripture for ourselves, and not rely on 'experts', 'the wise', 'teachers' or 'ministers'. This requires us to read the revelation of God with understanding. Then we will be in a position to recognize faithful teachers and seek out those who are wise in the Lord. At the Reformation, a very important teaching was brought to the fore. This was the priesthood of all believers. God has not set up a system where we approach him via human priests. This would undermine the finished work of Jesus Christ — who has offered the supreme sacrifice for sin and brings all who believe in him into God's presence. As priests, all the children of God are called to search the Scriptures and to receive God's Word. We are not left to do this on our own: we are to do it as people empowered and guided by the Spirit of Jesus. This is the privilege of all God's children (John 14:16-18; 1 Corinthians 3:11-13).

3. Scripture interprets itself

We can learn much by looking at the way Jesus and the Apostles used the Old Testament

EXPLANATION

Scriptures, including Genesis. This is God's way of teaching us the principles of interpretation. Indeed, this should be viewed as the primary way for us to learn: sitting at the feet of Jesus and those he has appointed to bring us inspired instruction.

PRACTICAL TASKS

Search the Scriptures for New Testament teaching on creation and origins

Genesis 1:	2 Corinthians 4:6; Hebrews 1:3
Genesis 2:	Matthew 19:4-5 (Mark 10:6-8); 1 Corinthians 15:45; 1 Timothy 2:13; Hebrews 4:4
Genesis 3:	John 8:44; Romans 5:12-19; Romans 8:20-22; 2 Corinthians 11:3
Genesis 4:	Luke 11:50-51; Hebrews 11:4; 1 John 3:12
Genesis 5:	Hebrews 11:5; Jude 14
Genesis 6:	Luke 17:26-27; Hebrews 11:7
Genesis 6-8:	1 Peter 3:20; 2 Peter 2:5.

In each case, consider how the Lord Jesus or the inspired writer used the text of Genesis. Is it possible to determine what type of literature they thought Genesis to be? Are these chapters viewed as poetry, prophecy, wisdom literature, history, or something else?

The book of Genesis is no stranger to controversy

EXPLANATION

For a long time, Genesis has been a battleground for scholars. We will consider one case from history, to draw some lessons and help us apply the principles outlined above. The case concerns the origin of writing, and whether Moses could have been the author of the first five books of the Bible, which are also known as the 'Five books of Moses'.

In the nineteenth century, a group of academics and theologians (collectively known as the 'Higher Critical' Movement) claimed that Genesis was written by several authors living at different times in the history of Israel and certainly not by Moses. These scholars agreed unanimously that writing was not known to Abraham, Isaac, Jacob and Moses. So, they inferred, the events and laws recorded in the five books of Moses must have been handed down by word of mouth and put together by scribes later in Israel's history.

This position continued to the turn of the century. H. Schultz, writing in 1893, made this assertion: 'of the legendary character of the pre-Mosaic narratives, the time of which they treat is sufficient proof. It was a time prior to all knowledge of writing.'[1]

Clay tablet with Sumerian cuneiform text

(© Copyright The British Museum)

Although tablets like these were known at the time, the critics regarded them as artistic engravings rather than a form of writing.

This show of strength gave Christian writers more than a few headaches. Although there is no direct reference to Moses being the human author of the first five books of the Bible, there is clear reference to Moses being literate. The Ten Commandments, for example, were written by God on tablets of stone. There are explicit references to Moses' writing: Exodus 17:14; Exodus 24; Numbers 33:2; Deuteronomy 27:2-3; Deuteronomy 31:9, 24. So Christians had to find a way to respond to the scholars who declared that it was foolishness to take the Bible as historical truth. These Christians wisely chose to affirm the accuracy of the Bible, even though they could not prove their point. In their commentaries, they would typically have an introduction which suggested that writing was not unknown to Moses, even though direct evidence was lacking.

Fifty years later, the situation looked completely different. It became clear that the Higher Critical Movement was born in ignorance. The findings of archaeology showed that the scholars had made innumerable fundamental mistakes. Writing was practised much earlier than they had thought. We can now look back over this period and realize that there was no need for Christians to be defensive.

With the discovery of thousands of clay tablets from Babylonia, with their strange inscriptions, came the doubts that their purpose was ornamental. Eventually, the breakthrough came with an ability to translate inscriptions from both Babylonia and Egypt. It was then obvious that writing was commonplace throughout the ancient world — right back to the beginning of civilization.

It was a difficult time for Bible teachers, and it took several generations before truth overcame error. The value of this history for us is that it illustrates the three principles of interpretation.

1. God speaks so that we can know what he is saying. The words of Scripture were actually straight-forward to interpret. Moses and the Israelites were literate and God made use of written words to communicate his commands. Christians were right to stay with this understanding and not to be deflected by influential scholars who declared otherwise.

2. Our sinfulness affects the way we think. The scholar P. J. Wiseman wrote: 'Notwithstanding the lack of knowledge which prevailed during the period, critical theories were being invented, and critics imagined themselves capable of determining what they imagined to be the literary conditions, or lack of them, appropriate to those times.'[2]

3. Scripture interprets itself. The New Testament refers to the Law as being given through Moses (Matthew 19:8; 2 Corinthians 3:15). These texts, and others, fully complement the conclusion drawn from the first principle.

P. J. Wiseman has a striking testimony at the end of his book. He quotes one of the most brilliant archaeologists of his day, representing one of the greatest universities in the world. 'I was brought up a "Higher Critic", and consequently disbelieved in the actual truth of the early narratives of the Bible. Since then I have deciphered thousands of tablets, and the more I learn, the more I believe the Bible to be true.'[3]

Application of the three principles of interpretation to origins

EXPLANATION

Step by step, the Higher Critical approach had to slowly retreat. Today, even some unbelieving scholars will acknowledge the unified structure and message of Genesis. However, since the early chapters of Genesis are deemed still to be mythical by the majority of scholars, the literature available on these chapters is of very mixed quality. Higher Criticism has not given up when it comes to understanding Genesis 1-11.

We are living today in a new transitional time. During the twentieth century, Darwinism became the unchallenged orthodoxy for scientists and many other scholars. Towards the end of the century, the number of dissident voices increased substantially, and we are now in a time when alternative approaches to Darwinism can be at

least spoken about without receiving gratuitous insults!
This is an opportunity for Christians to return to Genesis and read it without having to force the biblical
account to conform to the evolutionary approach.

Our goal is to understand and receive God's revelation about origins. It is a matter of discipleship that we
place ourselves under Christ's authority. P. J. Wiseman
has not only provided us with the case study used in
this chapter, but he also provides, in his conclusions,
words which provide a fitting conclusion here.

> The writers of the New Testament base important arguments and illustrations on the narratives
> of Genesis. These arguments and illustrations
> would be worse than useless, they would be misleading, apart from the fact that these narratives
> are based on historical facts. The testimony of our
> Lord Jesus Christ, the Son of God, to the narratives contained in Genesis is of greater value than
> all [other] evidence...[4]

QUESTIONS FOR DISCUSSION

1. *Does it matter what type of literature Genesis represents? What if it was poetry? or a vision of origins that
has no link with history? Would it make any difference
to the way we read Genesis, and to the way we read
the words of the Lord Jesus when he referred to
Genesis?*

DISCUSS IT

2. Imagine yourself living 150 years ago, when the Higher Critical Movement was dominant. How would you advise Christians to respond to the 'assured results of modern criticism'?

3. Think again about the testimony of the archaeologist: 'I was brought up a "Higher Critic", and consequently disbelieved in the actual truth of the early narratives of the Bible. Since then I have deciphered thousands of tablets, and the more I learn, the more I believe the Bible to be true.' What is your testimony about how you came to your present views of Genesis? What are you looking for from this guide to creation and origins?

THE GUIDE

CHAPTER TWO

THE NATURE OF GOD: CREATOR OF ALL THINGS

BIBLE READING

Isaiah 45:18-25

INTRODUCTION

When I was a teenager, science emerged as my major interest — with astronomy occupying much of my thoughts. A great deal of time was spent reading whatever I could find about the Moon, the planets and the stars. Many hours were spent gazing at the night sky through a small telescope. I knew all the constellations by name, and many of the brighter stars. The *Photographic Lunar Atlas* was one of my prize possessions.

I remember going to a public meeting in my home town organized by the local astronomical society. The speaker was a national figure and the author of many of the books I had devoured. The talk was good, but the only thing I can remember of the content relates to the question time after the talk! Someone asked the speaker whether his astronomical work influenced whether he believed in God. The answer gave me much to think about. The speaker said that when he looked through his telescope, at the distant objects in our own galaxy, at other galaxies in our local cluster and then at other galaxies in other clusters, he was overwhelmed with the immensity of it all. He had come to the conclusion that the universe was just too big to have been made. No being, he said, not even God, could have the power, the knowledge and the capability of creating it.

At that stage in my life I was not a Christian, although I had read the Bible and probably knew more than most teenagers about its message. I knew that the biblical writers thought about these things in a way exactly opposite to this speaker! When they looked at the immensity of what God had made, it made them recognize their total dependence on God and their folly of questioning his wisdom.

> 'I am the LORD,
> who has made all things,
> who alone stretched out the heavens,
> who spread out the earth by myself'
>
> (Isaiah 44:24).

> 'This is what the LORD says —
>   the Holy One of Israel, and its Maker:
> Concerning things to come,
>   do you question me about my children,
>   or give me orders about the work of my hands?
> It is I who made the earth
>   and created mankind upon it.
> My own hands stretched out the heavens;
>   I marshalled their starry hosts'
>
> (Isaiah 45:11-12).

ILLUSTRATION

*The Andromeda Galaxy, sister to our own
Milky Way galaxy*

(Image courtesy of NASA)

When an object the size of our own galaxy
becomes a barely visible and tiny object in the
night sky, the immensity of the universe comes
home to us. Yet the Bible teaches us that our God
has made all these things. It is a marvel that the
one who has such power and wisdom should
also stoop to communicate with ourselves —
who appear to be so insignificant. The practical
effect of this knowledge is to give believers a firm
conviction that our God reigns over all and
lacks no power to do whatever he wants to do.

The point about these reflections is that the sheer magnitude of the universe shapes our thinking about God. On the one hand, some conclude that it is just too large to have been made by anyone we might call God. On the other hand, we can conclude that if this is what God has made, how immense he must be! Anyone less than an all-powerful, all-wise being must be an invention of the human mind.

Creation out of nothing
(often referred to as 'Creation *ex nihilo*')

'In the beginning God created the heavens and the earth' (Genesis 1:1). This majestic declaration, in the first words of Scripture, informs us that God is the key to understanding origins. He speaks the word and brings the universe and all living things into existence. Before he spoke in this way, there was nothing that could be described as material — there was no universe! He has created out of nothing. This teaching is drawn from Genesis 1 and is declared many times in the Old Testament. For example, Isaiah 66:2 says, 'Has not my hand made all these things, and they came into being?' It is summarized in Hebrews 11:3: 'By faith we understand that the universe was formed at God's command, so that what is seen was not made out of what was visible.'

As we look around us, everything we see can be traced back to the creative genius of God. 'How many

EXPLANATION

are your works, O LORD! In wisdom you made them all' (Psalm 104:24).

This basic truth changes the way we view the world, because it means we live in a world that has direction. All things, whether animal, vegetable or mineral, have meaning and purpose because God is a personal being, who always acts in wisdom and according to his perfect plan. This is liberating, because we are not tiny specks of dust in a gigantic impersonal cosmic accident. It is challenging, because we cannot remain as observers — we ourselves are part of God's creation and we need to hear God's call, and then seek and find his purpose for our lives.

The biblical teaching is that God is altogether separate from the universe. He is the Creator and the cosmos is the created. This means that the material world is not a form of God. Many mystical religions elevate the world around us to divine status, a view that we call 'pantheism'. Needless to say, pantheism is alien to Scripture.

The Bible also speaks directly to our own culture, where it is widely held that the universe created itself. Many assert that it is unplanned, self-assembling and without purpose. This view is known as 'materialism', or 'naturalism'. Materialists have no place for God in their thinking and any attempt to attribute the origin of the universe to God is declared to be unscientific: an outdated 'creation myth'. Against this, the Bible declares that if we do not recognize God's creating power and purpose, our thinking is not just deficient, it is seriously astray.

A finished creation

God's creative activity took place in the six days of Creation Week. After this, we read that 'The heavens and the earth were completed in all their vast array. By the seventh day, God had finished the work he had been doing; so on the seventh day he rested from all his work' (Genesis 2:1-2).

Strange as it appears at first sight, the extraordinary activity of Creation Week reached its climax with God at rest. The significance of this will be considered in chapter 12, but here, we focus on creation as a 'completed' and 'finished' work.

Starting with Genesis 1, every reference to creation in the Bible is in the past tense. This is important: creating is not God's present activity, illustrated by the following testimonies from the Old Testament.

Moses (Psalm 90:2): 'Before the mountains were born or you brought forth the earth and the world, from everlasting to everlasting you are God.'

David (Psalm 24:2): 'For he [the LORD] founded it [the earth] upon the seas and established it upon the waters' (see also Psalm 136:1-9).

Solomon (Proverbs 8:22-31), *Isaiah* (Isaiah 42:5, 45:12) and *Jeremiah* (Jeremiah 10:12) all say similar things.

Simply drawing attention to the thought that creation is finished raises other questions about what God has been doing since then. This leads us to consider other parts of God's revelation. Although his rest relates to his creative activity, the Scriptures show that he is actively working in other ways.

God's continuing activity

When God created, was he acting like a master clockmaker who assembles a clock, winds it up and leaves it to run (knowing that it will keep perfect time)? Is the cosmos a gigantic machine, set up at the beginning and then allowed to run its course? There have been people who have thought like this. They were very influential in the past and gained the name 'deists'.

The Bible, however, has a completely different emphasis. God is no absentee landlord! The whole creation is totally dependent on God for its continuing existence. He upholds it. He sustains it. Without his mighty power, it would not continue to exist.

EXPLANATION

PRACTICAL TASKS

*Determine what the New Testament says about the
relationship between God and his creation. Consider
the following Scriptures.*

- John 1:1-3
- 1 Corinthians 8:6
- Hebrews 1:2-3
- Colossians 1:16-17
- Acts 14:15-17.

What do they teach about:

a. Christ's role in creation?
b. Christ's relationship to the creation now?
c. The power that goes forth from God to affect the creation?

The Old Testament also attributes every working of the
world about us directly to the hand of God. Thus, he
makes the grass grow; he makes the rain to fall; he feeds
the animals (Psalm 104:10-15). Since so much of our
experience of God's ongoing activity involves him pro-
viding for us (people) and for the other living things he
has made, a special term has been found. We refer to
this activity as his 'providence'. You can find the same
thought in Acts 14:15-17, when Barnabas and Paul
explained to the people of Lystra that God really had

showed them kindness. They said, 'He *provides* you with plenty of food and fills your hearts with joy.'

So, we have two terms to describe biblical teaching: 'creation', referring to his making of all things during Creation Week; and 'providence', referring to his upholding of the whole creation so that his creatures are fed and can fill the earth, as he had commanded. This teaching about the relationship between God and his creation is known as 'theism'.

Some have claimed that God's 'creation' and his 'providence' relate only to material things and that these activities do not involve miracles. The miraculous, they say, is reserved for his works of salvation. But this claim is contrived and arbitrary. There is no biblical distinction between the power God used to create material things and the power he uses to save his people (see Jeremiah 10:16; Romans 8:18-22; 2 Corinthians 4:6).

'Providence' and the rise of science

Historically, the period known as the 'Scientific Revolution' occurred in societies that were deeply influenced by the Christian faith. We shall examine whether this is significant. If it is, then science owes a debt of gratitude to Christianity for creating the cultural context that made it possible for science to thrive. Furthermore, those who present science as inherently in tension with Christianity are greatly misled.

Science did not come from societies influenced by animism, because their world is capricious, and inherently unpredictable. The 'spirits' of trees and stones are thought to exert influences that affect human life, and offerings must be made to gain their favour. Even sophisticated people can be affected by animism: we do not see these traits only in jungle-dwelling tribes. Animism affected the Greeks, despite their love of philosophy. They believed in many gods, who argued and fought among themselves and, in so doing, they affected human society. Whatever strengths the Greeks had, the culture was not supportive of the rise of science. There were a few that pioneered the way, but the significance of what they were doing was lost.

Other civilizations offered the potential for science to develop. The Chinese were technologically advanced well before the fourteenth century AD, but science eluded them. The Medieval Islamic culture was impressive, but a scientific community did not emerge. The reason is comparable to that for the Greeks: the culture was not right for science to flourish.

What was needed was, firstly, a positive theology of creation and providence. 'Creation' brings into focus a universe that was created according to the wisdom of God, and that declares his glory. 'Providence' brings a sense that all things are governed according to a wise plan, evidencing consistency, reliability and

EXPLANATION

predictability. Secondly, a community of people is needed that is prepared to experiment with the natural world, with the goal of understanding a little more of how God's creation works. This was the spirit of the pioneers of science in Europe, and the widespread Christian culture of the time was present to nurture science in its infancy.

What is 'science'?

This understanding of the world is foundational to science. Material things come from the hand of the Master Craftsman. Our world has an underlying design and it behaves predictably because God is the God of order. Science is a journey of exploration to bring us closer to 'thinking God's thoughts after him'. Scientific laws are the orderly patterns we discover by studying God's creation. The proper domain of science is the realm of God's providence — it describes the way God upholds his creation.

QUESTIONS FOR DISCUSSION

1. *Many people want to say that there must be a purpose behind everything, even though some leading scientists assure them that science can*

explain everything without the need to involve God. What Scriptures speak to these two groups? How can you help people to have confidence that the world is designed and that it does have a purpose?

2. *The Bible teaches 'theism', not 'pantheism', nor 'animism', nor 'deism'. Review the meaning of these terms and consider what the Bible has to say about each of them.*

3. *It is not unusual today to hear media figures speaking of science as though it was hostile to Christianity. How could you respond to such thinking? Explain the doctrine of providence by reference to Scripture and show its relevance.*

THE GUIDE

CHAPTER THREE

THE NATURE OF GOD: HE IS PERSONAL

LOOK IT UP

BIBLE READING

John 1:1-14

INTRODUCTION

Parenthood is an extraordinary blessing from God. Surely every parent knows something of the richness of Solomon's words: 'Sons are a heritage from the LORD, children a reward from him' (Psalm 127:3). After the pains of labour and childbirth, it is an unparalleled emotional relief to cuddle the newborn child and sense the peace the baby experiences. Then, hour by hour, one gets to know the new person that has come into the family. The baby learns how to express itself, even though it takes about a year before words are spoken. After about eight weeks, facial muscles are developed sufficiently for the baby to smile, and this brings with it many new opportunities for non-verbal communication!

The child takes pleasure in light, sound and touch. Parents realize that consciousness, or self-awareness, is with the child at birth. It is not something infused into the child by the environment. The child is a *person* at birth (indeed, personality traits make themselves known in the womb!). Parenting involves nurturing a *person* from an initial state of total dependence to when that individual can act as an independent adult.

Every newborn baby is a person. This infant is less than an hour old, still in the hospital delivery room, and is having a good look at his dad.

The experience of parenthood helps us understand what it is to be a person. Persons can communicate, and speech is uniquely human. Words are not only used to express needs or to sound an alarm, but also can convey ideas, describe and interpret past events, and be used in an infinite number of other ways. Additionally, people have an appreciation of the world around them: its beauty and its grandeur. Furthermore, people can interact with the world by making things and moulding the environment to make it 'home'. They are creative.

Supremely, people are self-aware. We know that we are individuals and different from other individuals. We show this by each having a personal name and we act consciously instead of by instinct. We have a conscience, so that we know right from wrong and what we ought to do. We can put ourselves in the shoes of others, understanding their ambitions and feeling something of their pain. This level of consciousness is a notable human trait. By contrast, the animals are ruled by instinct and do not enter the world of imaginations, ideas and morality.

God is personal

The first recorded words of speech in the Bible are 'Let there be light' (Genesis 1:3). God speaks many times in Genesis 1 — he uses words to express his will. Since he is all powerful, it is enough for him to speak and it is done (Psalm 33:9).

Repeatedly, we read 'God saw that it was good', indicating that he recognizes beauty and finds worth in the things he has made. Thus, aesthetic appreciation is part of God's character.

God is said to have 'blessed' the living things in the sea and in the air (Genesis 1:22), indicating that he takes an interest in them and their future. He is not distant .from the works of his hands. He points to outcomes of his creative work with which he is pleased.

God also said, 'Let us make man in our image, in our likeness.' These words indicate consultation prior to making the first man and woman. Since God is a unity (there is one God), these words are remarkable. They express divine counsel and self-communion.

Significantly, in Genesis 2, God goes on to communicate with man. He is a personal Creator and able to stoop to communicate with the people he has made. He chooses to reveal himself to man. As finite creatures, we cannot hope to know God in the infinity of his being, but we can know him as a person when he reveals himself to us.

God is no stranger to the qualities we have come to associate with personal relationships. The Bible makes it clear that this is not a case of man creating a god to worship that has human traits. On the contrary, human traits are what they are because we are made in God's image (Genesis 1:26-27). How can these things be? God is a spiritual being, and spiritual beings are persons. Man is unique among living things on Earth, for only he has a material body and a spiritual essence. Man therefore is a spiritual being and this is why we also are persons, capable of knowing our Maker.

Determine what the New Testament says about the personal nature of God, particularly in relation to creation.

Consider the following Scriptures:

John 1:1-14: Who is the 'Word'? What is the connection between the 'Word' and creation? What indications are there that the 'Word' is personal?

Romans 1:18-25: What does the creation reveal about God's 'invisible qualities'? Why is it wrong for man to make images that 'look like mortal man and birds and animals and reptiles'? What is the 'truth of God' that is exchanged for a lie when people worship idols?

Colossians 1:14-18: What does Paul mean when he writes that the Son is 'the image of the invisible God'? What does this teach us about the personal nature of God? Jesus Christ is Lord in relation to the church, but why is it also important for him to be Lord over creation?

Hebrews 1:1-4: How do the actions and words described in this passage inform us about the 'being' of the Son and the 'being' of God?

We see in Genesis 1-3, and in the above New Testament Scriptures, God's personal nature. As a person, he has chosen to communicate, and does indeed communicate, not only with angels but also with man. This is termed 'revelation'. God *reveals* his word to mankind. He communicates truth. He makes known his will. He explains his purpose. It is obvious from the Bible that God has many things to say to mankind. It is also obvious, as seen in every book of the Bible, that the root problem is not God speaking, but man listening! Adam and his wife 'hid from the LORD God' as soon as they had disobeyed his command (Genesis 3:8), and their descendants have done much the same ever since.

Many people struggle with the thought that God reveals himself and his will. They insist that God has not spoken to them. The writer to the Hebrews gives us the correct perspective by which to understand their attitudes. God has spoken 'at many times and in various ways' (Hebrews 1:1), but supremely, 'he has spoken to us by his Son'. The message was announced by the Lord and confirmed by those who had been with him. Yet further testimony was given by 'signs, wonders and various miracles' and by the 'gifts of the Holy Spirit' (Hebrews 2:3-4). There is enough here for anyone! 'See to it that you do not refuse him who speaks' (Hebrews 12:25). When Jesus told the story of the rich man and Lazarus, he made a very similar point: 'If they do not listen to Moses and the Prophets, they will not be convinced even if someone rises from the dead' (Luke

EXPLANATION

16:19-31). And, of course, his words were vindicated when he did rise from the dead and still the people did not listen.

Human beings have no reason to complain because this message is 2000 years old. God is not like a man, rethinking his words and revising his plans. There is a partial unveiling of truth in the Old Testament, but the whole emphasis of the New Testament is that in Christ God's revelation of himself is complete. The task of each generation is to receive these abiding truths and to apply them to present situations. Two thousand years of church history have shown, not only that this is possible, but also that the commission we have from the Lord really is exciting and challenging.

Revealed truth is knowledge to be prized above all else. Believers can say, with the psalmist: 'How sweet are your words to my taste, sweeter than honey to my mouth!' (Psalm 119:103). Revealed truth is *certain* knowledge. It is not like the words of men, because God always speaks the truth and he does not deceive us (1 Thessalonians 2:13). It is worth comparing this with scientific truth, which is always partial and may be mixed up with error.

Furthermore, revealed truth is not difficult to acquire. God's Word is not inaccessible. He does not require us to pass exams before we are capable of receiving truth. We can have a sense of assurance whenever we hear, understand and re-spond to the Word of God. If our reading of the Bible leaves us in a state of confusion, then we have lost the plot. We need to restore the spirit of discipleship. This involves coming to God in dependence, 'like a little child' (Luke 18:17). Believers are to be *child-like* in our relationship with our heavenly Father (not *childish*, as some have mistakenly thought).

Does God's truth really bring us knowledge?

How do we handle the subject of origins? Our culture is hostile to the very thought of 'revealed truth'. Intel-lectual leaders deny that there can be any knowledge that is revealed and, at best, they allow 'religion' to be a private matter. They refuse to allow the Bible to have any influence in schools and universities, in the sciences or in the humanities. Intellectual life is made a 'no go' area for biblical teaching — which is allowed only in religious studies. Anything more than this is opposed by talk of 'grave concerns' about 'Christian fundamen-talists' who have given up on the use of reason.

However, privatizing religion makes all beliefs rela-tive. They are 'true' only for the individual. This suits the intellectual leaders who want to make 'knowledge' exclusive to science. They drive a wedge between revelation and knowledge. They say that only science can yield knowledge, although some will allow revelation a place in the context of subjective experience. This means that different people can have different religious experiences and can hold different beliefs — but that does not matter, say these leaders, because these beliefs are 'true' for each individual believer.

The Bible teaches otherwise! The purest knowledge we have is revealed by God. This is knowledge we can rely on. It is a foundation on which we can build. We have already noted in chapter 2 that the Bible is foundational to the sciences. We shall see in chapter 4 that the Bible is foundational for every area of human thought. Bible-believing Christians seek to place Christ and biblical revelation at the centre of our intellectual lives, and this puts us out of step with the world around us. We must either 'grasp the nettle' and stand against the tide of opinion, or succumb. This is the challenge felt by any disciple of Christ who wants to respond to Paul's exhortation to be 'transformed by the renewing of your mind' (Romans 12:2).

A major area of relevance for us is origins. There are many who tell us that science informs us 'how', whereas religion explores the question 'Why?' This popular approach perpetuates the myths that knowledge comes only from science, and that revelation deals exclusively with questions of meaning and purpose. The simple reason why this whole approach is unbiblical is that the Bible provides us with a history of origins as well as bringing teaching about the meaning of it all. History does not make science redundant, but it certainly provides answers to 'how' questions and consequently establishes constraints for scientific quest.

Without history, there are many possible explanations that might appeal to us. To recognize the significance of this, we can consider the discipline of archaeology. Researchers document their findings in meticulous detail, and engage in extensive debate as to what the observations mean. Because scholars have inventive minds, the same data can lead to radically different interpretations of past events. Reliable history is actually a welcome constraint for archaeologists. They do not regard history as an unwelcome intrusion into their discipline. They recognize that reliable historical records save them from wasting their time on speculation, allowing them to reach robust conclusions that are satisfying. In this way there is a genuine advance in knowledge.

This is the contribution of biblical history: it constrains science and advances knowledge. It is in no way hostile to science, although it may offend those who are wedded to their own speculations as to what any data means.

A good example of this concerns the beginnings of the Christian Church. There have always been numerous unconvincing explanations of how demoralized and traumatized disciples turned into fearless apostles who turned the world upside down. The only convincing explanation is the one illuminated by biblical history. Jesus actually did rise from the dead and appeared to his followers.

In a culture that denies God, it is necessary to postulate a creation that made itself. We must live in a self-assembling universe where life emerged from chemicals, where simple living things evolved into complex organisms, and where the evolutionary process culminated in intelligent life. It is vital to our culture that this evolution occurred without a guiding or controlling hand. Advocates of this approach can cope with differences of view about the mechanisms, but there can be no compromise on the general principle. Evolution must have occurred, they argue, as a matter of necessity.

Suffice to say here that this evolutionary history is radically different from biblical history. We shall consider this further in chapter 7. However, for the present, it is suggested that biblical revelation, and specifically biblical history, are important contributions to the thinking of anyone who wants to know what really happened 'in the beginning'.

QUESTIONS FOR DISCUSSION

1. *What does the Bible say about what it is to be a person? How would you explain to someone that cats and dogs are not persons but babies are?*

2. *How would you explain to someone that God is a person? What does the Bible have to say about this?*

3. *Does God's revealed truth count as knowledge? Does God's truth extend to topics outside matters of salvation? What passages of the Bible could you use to help people who struggle with this issue?*

4. *Genesis 5 records details of people who lived before the Flood, most of whom lived for about 900 years. Is it reasonable to think that this historical data might helpfully inform and constrain scientific thinking about ageing?*

CHAPTER FOUR

HUMANITY BEARS THE IMAGE OF GOD

LOOK IT UP

BIBLE READING

Psalm 8

INTRODUCTION

Long ago, a shepherd sat in the open air, the stars above his head, reflecting on the meaning of life. In his heart, he communed with the Lord, the Creator of all he could see around him. He considered how extraordinary it is for people to have a relationship with the living God. 'What is man', he thought, 'that you are mindful of him?' (Psalm 8:4).

He knew that sheep live much, much simpler lives. Give them green pastures and access to fresh water and they are content! Men and women are not like this. For some, life is an adventure; for others, it is a maze; for others still, it is a journey full of sorrows and tears. Man lives at a level that is quite different from that of animals. We speak about our feelings and emotions; we can create a world in our minds; we have memories of the past, and hopes and fears for the future.

The shepherd David must have reflected often on what the Scriptures say about this, as we should also if we seek wisdom. One passage in the creation account is particularly relevant. Genesis 1:27 teaches us that man is different from the animals — nothing else in creation was created in the image of God. We know from the second commandment (Exodus 20:4) that the making of any image of God is something to be deplored. Idolatry is a crime against our Maker that calls down his judgements upon those who practise it. We are not to make any images of God, yet here in the very first chapter of the Bible, we are told that God made mankind in his own image. How can it be possible for finite man to be the image of the eternal, infinite God?

What does this image-bearing mean? We need some guidance if we are to answer this question. The principles we met in chapter 1 are relevant here, particularly 'Scripture interprets itself'. Using this principle we can ask: 'What are those aspects of humanity that are associated with image-bearing?'

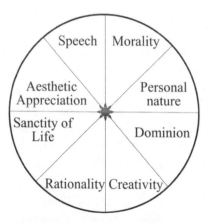

Eight dimensions of image-bearing

EXPLANATION

We have seen in chapter 2 that God is the Creator and, because he is an infinite spiritual being, finite creatures cannot image this aspect of his nature. We have also seen, in chapter 3, that he is a personal spiritual being. At this level, we can be like him. And if we are personal spiritual beings ourselves, we can have a meaningful relationship with God. This is where we must seek the meaning of 'image-bearing'. We use the principle of Scripture interpreting Scripture to help us understand what God is revealing of himself in the way he has created mankind, as shown below.

- *Speech*: We speak because God speaks. In Genesis 1, God speaks repeatedly. In Genesis 2, God speaks to Adam and Adam speaks to God. The contrast with animals is total. Psalm 19 exults in the fact that God communicates with us. Proverbs 2 points to God's words as the source of wisdom for us, so that we can become wise also.
- *Morality*: We are to obey God and be holy because God is our Master and he is holy (Leviticus 19:1). God's right to place obligations on Adam and Eve is apparent in Genesis 1-2.
- *Personal nature*: We have looked at this matter already in chapter 3. Persons are able to enter into relationships. Genesis 1:26 records the Lord saying, 'Let us make man in our image.' This divine consultation regarding the

creation of humankind suggests that God was no stranger to personal relationships prior to creation. He was not lonely before he created man. God made Adam and also gave him a wife as his companion and helper. We are not meant to be individualists, but those who develop meaningful relationships with other people as well as with God. In Genesis 3:8-9, we read of God's relationship with Adam and his wife. After they disobeyed, they hid. When the Lord did not find them, he called out, 'Where are you?' Such questions are addressed to our consciences, which we have because we are spiritual personal beings.

- *Dominion*: We have dominion because God is the Ruler of all. Genesis 1:26-28 refers explicitly to rule over the animals and the Earth. There is also the command to subdue the Earth. Psalm 8:6-8 draws from these words in Genesis. We shall consider the implications of dominion in chapters 10 and 11.

- *Creativity*: We create because God creates. Man's creativity emerges very quickly in biblical history. In Genesis 4 we read of people building cities, making and playing musical instruments, and working with bronze and iron.

- *Rationality* (the ability to reason and think logically): We are rational because God is rational. Genesis 1-3 reveals not only God's rational communication, but also man's. After sin entered, human rationality became compromised as blame was passed and weak excuses were invented in an attempt to escape the feeling of guilt. We are not like the 'unreasoning animals' (Jude 10).

EXPLANATION

- *Sanctity of life*: We are precious because God is precious. Abel's death was a solemn and serious matter: 'Your brother's blood cries out to me from the ground' (Genesis 4:10). The mark of Cain (v. 15) was given to stop other descendants of Adam and Eve taking vengeance on him. Jesus' life is of infinite value because he is truly man and truly God (Hebrews 10:11-14). The death of animals is portrayed quite differently in the Scriptures.
- *Aesthetic appreciation*: We appreciate beauty and design because this mirrors God's character. In Genesis 1:31, the Lord declared all that he had made to be 'very good'. In 2:9, God made trees that were pleasing to the eye as well as being good for food. There were other lovely things in Eden (2:12). It is significant that the first person in the Bible who is mentioned as being filled with the Spirit of God was Bezalel (Exodus 31:2-3). He had skill, ability and knowledge in all kinds of craft and design work.

To know that we bear the image of God is revolutionary! It is a transforming truth. We could never know it for sure without revelation, although we might suspect that the profound differences between ourselves and animals must have an explanation! This truth should affect every aspect of our lives and every area of thought.

The consequences to society of denying image-bearing

The biblical teaching about man's uniqueness stands in sharp contrast to much thinking today which portrays man as just another animal. In popular parlance, he is a naked but intelligent ape. This view has cheapened life in every one of the eight dimensions of image-bearing.

PRACTICAL TASKS

Use the 'eight dimensions' illustration to help analyse social trends. In the list below, which aspects of image-bearing are under attack?

- widespread use of swearing and oaths in television and films (see James 3:9)
- the meaninglessness of 'modern' art
- curiosity about and fascination with astrology and horoscopes
- the breakdown of family life
- the explosion of pornography
- exploitation of workers, including children, especially in developing countries
- terrorism
- abortion, infanticide, euthanasia, human cloning
- increasing destruction of natural environments
- the drug culture

EXPLANATION

The only rational basis for challenging these trends (as distinct from having a gut feeling about them) is to base our arguments on man being made in God's image. Without this foundation, we cannot say anything with confidence. The world's experts increasingly avoid talking about truth and error, right and wrong. They limit their role to analysing the opinions of leaders, because they recognize there is no authority behind any of them. We need to pray for Christians who can minister to our generation, who seek to bring God's truth to hurting people. God has given us answers; we need to apply them.

Evolutionary views of human origins

Genesis 2 teaches us that God formed Adam from the dust of the ground and then breathed life into him. Adam became a 'living being' (v. 7). Genesis also describes the animals as 'living creatures' (v. 19). Both man and the air-breathing animals had 'the breath of life' (Genesis 2:7; 7:21-22). Adam, therefore, was not an animal before he became a 'living being'. His creation should not be interpreted as God breathing life into a pre-existent ape. Forming his body was a miraculous event. We also read of Eve's creation from a part of Adam. Her body did not come from an animal and she also had a miraculous origin. Mankind is a 'special' creation.

God made Adam and Eve from the outset to have the characteristics we recognize as 'advanced'. They spoke words and reasoned both with each other and with God. They were intelligent; for example, Adam named the animals (Genesis 2:20). Furthermore, their immediate descendants were arable and livestock farmers and Cain, Adam's eldest son, was the first to build a city. Later descendants worked with metals and made music (Genesis 4:21-22).

The story of human origins that we are told by the evolutionists is that ape-like animals became more man-like over the past few million years, developed the ability to walk on two legs and started making very simple stone tools. With the passing of time, animals looking very similar to man became conscious of their individuality, made complex stone tools and started to take an interest in what happens after death. This led to Modern Man appearing in the later parts of the Old Stone Age, still a hunter/gatherer but with a flowering of artistic ability. In the New Stone Age, man became a farmer and built houses (and cities). Only after this were the skills developed so that man could work with metals. This cultural evolution extends over thousands of years. There is thus a clear tension between what we know of 'early man' from the Bible and this widely accepted account of human evolution.

Some Christians have tried to reinterpret the evolutionary story using biblical terminology. So, for example, some have suggested that the appearance of the New Stone Age farmers marks the generations of people immediately following Adam and Eve. In this view, God breathed his image into a pre-human Stone Age man (and woman). This then triggered the novelties of the New Stone Age (the Neolithic Revolution). Others have suggested that God breathed his image into a even earlier pre-human. This is because religious burial, artistry and musical ability are regarded as human qualities apparent in the Old Stone Age. Like so many attempts to reconcile the Bible with evolutionary stories, these interpretations pick on a few points of apparent agreement but neglect the broader issues. None of these attempted reconciliations have stood up to the test of criticism and it is time they were abandoned.

We need a different approach. We have seen in chapter 1 that the early chapters of Genesis are as much history as the later chapters. Adam and Eve, Cain and Abel, Jabal and Jubal were all real people. Human culture was advanced at the outset. It could degenerate to the level of Old Stone Age man, but it did not evolve from it. Starting with this framework of truth, we need to look afresh at the findings of archaeology.

Concluding comments

Without God's revelation, human nature is a total mystery. Why are we so different from the animals? Genetically, we are very similar to chimpanzees, but in all other respects there is a great gulf between apes and man. Bridging the gap has been the ambition of many materialists, particularly in the area of science. The Nobel prize winner Francis Crick has been in the news in 2003 because of the fiftieth anniversary of the discovery of DNA's structure. He is quoted as saying that his distaste for religion was one of his prime motives in the work that led to the sensational 1953 discovery. 'I went into science because of these religious reasons, there's no doubt about that. I asked myself what were the two things that appear inexplicable and are used to support religious beliefs: the difference between living and nonliving things, and the phenomenon of consciousness.'[1] Crick considers that the DNA work closes the gap between life and non-life, and much of the latter part of his life has been devoted to finding a materialist explanation of the soul.

Quests like these are doomed to failure. The essence of life is biological information, not the DNA molecule that is, at best, a sophisticated carrier. The essence of consciousness is not physics and chemistry, but image-bearing. We are spiritual beings, and materialistic analysis must always be deficient. We need to build science on a better foundation than materialism, and that foundation is provided by the revelation of God.

QUESTIONS FOR DISCUSSION

DISCUSS IT

1. What does the Bible mean when it describes man as being made in God's image (Genesis 1:27)? Why are we different from animals, which are also 'living beings'? What are the key biblical verses that we need to refer to if we are to share these truths with others?

2. In this chapter, image-bearing is described as a transforming truth. Can you recall situations where the knowledge of being made in the image of God made a real difference to you? Can you find this truth in Matthew 6:25-34 and 22:20?

3. Look again at the Practical Tasks, this time within a group, if possible. Making use of past issues of national newspapers, find stories that illustrate other social trends. Discuss how these relate to the eight dimensions of image-bearing. You will certainly find examples of divisions in society. Read Colossians 3:9-11 and consider what image-bearing means when we are in Christ.

4. How has the evolutionary story of human origins affected you? Read Romans 5:12-21 and ask what happens to Paul's argument if death was the universal experience of Adam's evolutionary ancestors? How will you react next time you meet with the 'evolution of man' story on television, video or in literature?

CHAPTER FIVE

THE NATURE OF MAN: DISOBEDIENT AND REBELLIOUS

BIBLE READING

Romans 5:12-19

INTRODUCTION

About 250 years ago, it was fashionable to think that we should look to primitive peoples to find a purer way of life. There were imagined to be distant tribes, untainted by the tough, brutal culture of so-called civilized man. The 'noble savage' concept was the brainchild of a Frenchman called Jean Jacques Rousseau. His 'romantic' dream proved to be very influential in society and many came to share his idealistic vision. Explorers actually went out to areas remote from civilization to search for tribes who lived in peace and harmony, yet were free from the framework of law and morality that characterizes civilized societies. Claims were soon made that there were tribes who fitted the 'noble savage' description. The first and most celebrated 'paradise' was Tahiti, and many stories were told of this 'Eden' in the Pacific. However, subsequent investigations revealed a rather different picture: these tribes were, in fact, no more noble than ourselves. The communities that outsiders claimed

were harmonious and peaceful were really just like the
rest of human society.

The human enigma

Historically, the romantic vision of human nature was
a response to the idea that man was a tiny cog in a
gigantic impersonal machine. Prior to Rousseau and
other pioneers of Romanticism, the period known as
the Enlightenment had gained the allegiance of many
intellectual leaders. Their favoured way of describing
the universe was to represent it as an elaborate machine. This approach claimed to build on the Scientific Revolution that had preceded it, drawing particularly on the mechanical theories of Isaac Newton.

However, whereas the early scientists had been
theists, the Enlightenment scholars were rationalists.
Their 'world' was constructed by the exclusive use of
their powers of reason. It emerged as impersonal and
hostile: one where man was an enigma. Yet man did
not fit into the Enlightenment world because we do
not behave like machines. We are conscious beings who
know right and wrong and who often choose the wrong.

The Romantics found a greater affinity with the idea
that the world is an organism (rather than a mechanism). When man behaves as though he is part of the
organism, they thought, there is harmony and beauty.
By returning to our roots, paradise can be restored. This
motivated the search for the 'noble savage'.

Romanticism did not want man to be a cog in the Cosmic Machine — but how could a place be found where humans could feel at home?

Romanticism is with us today (as we shall see in chapter 11), though its cultural roots have changed. Today, there is enormous disillusionment with the human race and its technological achievements. There are many reasons for feeling downcast, in addition to the thought that humans are mere cogs in a giant machine. We do not have to look very hard before we see injustice, oppression, exploitation, violence, lust, unfaithfulness, wars, pollution and extinction. Why do humans cause so many problems? Why is this sad story so similar, generation after generation? In the face of such overwhelming evidence, it is hard to be optimistic about the future of humanity.

How do we explain the human condition? We've tried education, but that just produces intelligent oppressors and clever law-breakers. We've tried a harder line on policing, but that just increases the prison population. We've tried giving people a higher standard of living, but people respond by wanting more and more material things and still they are not satisfied. We've tried to blame religious superstition and created a 'secular' society, but the problems are increasing. Where should we look next? Should we really be searching for yet another scapegoat? Confusion abounds!

Man is dead

Genesis 3 is arguably one of the most important chapters in the Bible! We learn here that there was an original paradise: the Garden of Eden. We learn that our first parents were free from all those moral failures that mar our relationships today. We learn how this changed when sin entered the world by an act of disobedience. It was a remarkable transformation!

How was it possible for Adam and Eve, created holy and pure, to disobey God? Although this question is not simple to answer, the Bible presents the option of disobedience plainly, in a matter-of-fact way. God said to Adam, 'You must not eat from the tree of the

EXPLANATION

knowledge of good and evil, for when you eat of it you will surely die' (Genesis 2:17). This was a command from God that Adam understood, and Eve's knowledge of it appears to have come through her husband.

The temptation to disobey God came through the serpent's words. Eve was deceived before she went against God's command, but not Adam (1 Timothy 2:14). He chose to disobey. This is how sin came into the world. This is how we define sin. It is disobedience to God. It is rebellion against his authority. It is falling short of God's standard of righteousness.

There are mysteries here, for how could a pure and sinless man ever rebel against God? The explanation must involve man being a free agent. Whether we are holy and pure, or whether we are lawbreakers and defiled, we make choices. Decisions are not made for us. We are conscious beings. Animals are not like this for they act by instinct. Their responses are not rational, in the sense that they do not go through a process of weighing reasons for acting in a certain way. These thoughts take us back to image-bearing, a topic we considered in chapter 4 of this guide. We are free agents because we are made in the image of God and have a personal nature.

Adam's sin had the consequence of alienation. Adam was alienated from God and God was alienated from man. Death was the punishment for sin, and death came upon all men (Romans 5:12). Furthermore, the broken relationship with God affected man's relationship to himself, to his fellow man and to the rest of creation. There can be no 'noble savages' today, because the damage has already been done. Sin has transformed the human condition. There are no isolated pockets of purity remaining.

Man's inner isolation leads to deep-seated psychological problems. Man's alienation from his fellow men leads to profound sociological problems. The broken relationship with the rest of creation brings environmental tragedy. If there is to be any hope for the human condition, it must come from God's goodwill towards man.

Spiritual and physical death

Spiritual death is essentially alienation from God. The day Adam sinned, he was cast out of Eden and he no longer lived in the presence of God (Genesis 3:23-24). This is the death spoken of by the apostle Paul to the Ephesian Christians when he said, 'You were dead in your transgressions and sins' (Ephesians 2:1). Physically they were alive, yet they were dead before God.

Neither Adam nor Eve died physically on the day they sinned. Nevertheless, we should note that Adam's physical death is part of the Edenic curse in Genesis 3:19. God said, 'For dust you are and to dust you will return.' Physical death then became the human experience. The refrain 'and he died' in Genesis 5 hammers home the message that physical death comes to us all. Enoch's translation in Genesis 5:24 stands out as a remarkable contrast. This man did not die physically but went to be with God. In the goodness of God, the ancients had this testimony to show them that death's power was not so strong that God could not triumph over it.

Romans 5:12-21 is a very significant New Testament commentary on the death that came through Adam. Paul refers repeatedly to physical death. 'Nevertheless, death reigned from the time of Adam to the time of Moses, even over those who did not sin by breaking a command' (v. 14). This verse is incomprehensible if 'death' is spiritual only. The 'death' referred to was visible. People were seen to die in the period between Adam and Moses, even though the Mosaic Law was not given. Indeed, infants also were known to have died — and they 'did not sin by breaking a command'. Furthermore, this section, and the subsequent passage in 6:1-14, draws a direct analogy between the sin of Adam bringing physical and spiritual death and the righteousness of Christ (in dying on the cross) where he experienced both physical and spiritual death on behalf of all who were to believe in him.

Without this understanding of death, the cross of Christ becomes an enigma. Unless physical death is the punishment of sin, there was no reason for Christ to have died physically. Unless spiritual death is the punishment of sin, Christ did not have to cry out, 'My God, my God, why have you forsaken me?' (Matthew 27:46). The Lord Jesus had prayed in the Garden of Gethsemane, 'My Father, if it is possible, may this cup be taken from me' (Matthew 26:39). There was no other way — otherwise the Father would have granted the Son's agonized request. To bear the punishment of sin, Christ had both to die physically and also to endure alienation from the Father.

PRACTICAL TASKS

Read Romans 6:1-23 and examine what the apostle Paul says about the link between death and sin.

• Baptism into Jesus Christ has a symbolic meaning. Baptism signifies being united with Christ in his death and resurrection (vv. 3-10). Is Paul here referring to Christ's physical death, spiritual death, or both? Explain what the symbol means and how it relates to us as believers.

• Paul describes slavery to sin and slavery to righteousness (vv. 15-18). Verse 21 says that the things you are now ashamed of 'result in death'; verse 23 declares that 'the wages of sin is death'. Is Paul thinking here of physical death, spiritual death or both?

Human origins and physical death

EXPLANATION

Physical death is not 'normal' for mankind. It is an ugly intrusion. Those of us who have watched loved ones die have witnessed something that mars the created order. If we are wise, we will not complain to God that he has made things this way. Rather, we will mourn the sin that has spoiled the joy of creation and brought such heart-ache and sorrow. Once we accept that physical death is a consequence of sin, there are significant implications for our understanding of the creation of Adam.

As we have already noted, many Christians today think that God breathed spiritual life into a pre-human animal. This allows them to accept evolutionary accounts of human origins from ape-like ancestors. The imparting of spiritual life is generally perceived as a miraculous intervention superimposed on a non-miraculous evolutionary transformation. Under this scheme, it follows that God used the cycle of reproduction and physical death to bring the body of Adam into existence.

However, if physical death is a punishment for sin, we cannot also teach that physical death was experienced by all of Adam's ancestors. 'The creation of man', as recorded in the Bible, was a direct act of God, using the dust of the ground. Only after Adam's disobedience was physical death part of the human experience.

The intellectual culture that dominates our own society considers man to be an evolved ape-like animal. Man, it is said, has not 'fallen' from a state of fellowship with God. He has emerged from a lifestyle governed by instinct to one where there is self-consciousness. There are big issues here for the terminology Christians use. When we speak of people being 'brought back to God', we understand that there is a restoration and an enhancement of the relationship Adam and Eve had with God in the beginning. Those who hear our words, however, belong to a different culture. They know nothing of an initial state when our first parents enjoyed the presence of God. They know nothing of a fall into a state of alienation. They know nothing about death being the punishment for sin. Christ has called us to take the gospel to the whole world, but how do we make sure that our words are not misunderstood or considered irrelevant by unbelievers?

QUESTIONS FOR DISCUSSION

1. *Christians share the Lord's Supper together, eating the bread and drinking the wine. What does the bread symbolize and what does the wine signify? Read 1 Corinthians 10:16-17. If physical death is not one of the consequences of sin, what becomes of Paul's words in 1 Corinthians 11:26: 'For whenever you eat this bread and drink this cup, you proclaim the Lord's death until he comes.'*

2. People with a Christian background are often so accustomed to thinking about mankind as alienated from God (because of sin) that we find it difficult to relate to people who have different backgrounds. Discuss cases known to you where you have sought to witness to people whose culture has no place for God. What brings about a conviction of sin and breaks through these cultural barriers to communication? How can 1 Corinthians 9:20-21 be applied to this situation?

3. Have you had to face the death of a loved one? Is death a normal part of God's creation? Or is death something that spoils creation? How can the answers to these questions be used to help those who mourn?

THE GUIDE

CHAPTER SIX

CURSING OF THE CREATED ORDER: THE CONSEQUENCES OF SIN

LOOK IT UP

BIBLE READING

Genesis 3:14-19

INTRODUCTION

One of the saddest conversations I can remember was with a mother who was very bitter in her feelings towards God. She was resolute in her rejection of everything to do with God, because she felt an unbearable pain within. Her hostility arose because her baby daughter had died many years before. She could not cope with the thought that God could allow such a thing to happen. She had been wrestling with the 'problem of pain', as have many others over the years.

The problem can be stated simply. If God is sovereign and Lord of all (which is the traditional Christian teaching), then he oversees and controls both the good and the bad in this world. Some people then argue that he is responsible in some way for everything — including the pain of suffering and death. They conclude that he cannot be a God of love and that he is a tyrant who does not care about people at all. This basic problem leads others to the opinion that God is not sovereign and that he merely observes but does not govern evil. There are still other reactions that we do not need to review. The important point for us is this: How does the Bible handle this situation? Is God really the author of evil?

Of course, the answer is no! God is holy and cannot look upon sin; and yet he is Lord of all. This message is brought home to us time after time in the Old Testament Scriptures. The problem of pain was certainly known to the people of God in those times. Indeed, it could be said to be the theme of the prophecies of Habakkuk. One of his complaints was that the wicked triumph over those more righteous than themselves. How could God let this happen when 'your eyes are too pure to look on evil' (Habakkuk 1:13)? You can read the answer the prophet received from God in Habakkuk 2. In the New Testament, the apostle Paul addresses this issue in Romans 9:17-29.

The creation, as it came from God's hands, was free from sin. Adam and Eve did not have to grapple with the 'problem of pain' in the Garden of Eden! The problem only arose after Adam sinned and God's judgements fell. It is to this momentous event in the Earth's history that we now turn.

Adam's sin and the Edenic curse
(Genesis 3)

If the dominion given to man is an aspect of image-bearing (as noted in chapter 4), then we must expect that the relationship between mankind and the rest of creation was affected by the entrance of sin. Instead of 'tending the garden', mankind exploits it. Instead of subduing the Earth, mankind pollutes, neglects and destroys it. These aspects of the breakdown of relations between man and creation are considered further in chapter 11.

When Adam disobeyed the command of God, the consequences were far-reaching. Everything was affected. The transformation is recorded in Genesis chapter 3, where God speaks words of judgement on the serpent, the woman and Adam.

Genesis 3:17-19 records some very significant pronouncements by the LORD God. The judgement of God upon the ground is declared: 'Cursed is the ground because of you.' This is far more than God recognizing that mankind would fail to look after creation. These words show that the marks of God's judgements on sin were then impressed on creation itself. This is the implication of the ground becoming cursed. Working the garden was to become 'painful toil'. Thorns and thistles would compete with food crops. Man's life would be characterized by sweat, and this situation would continue until his physical death.

The ground 'will produce thorns and thistles for you'
(Genesis 3:18)

The world changed when Adam sinned. The work that God gave was originally deeply satisfying and not burdensome. In tending the garden, Adam did not have to engage in painful toil. He was free to eat fruit (Genesis 2:16) and he was also given seed-bearing plants to eat (1:29). In Eden, we infer that crops did not compete with thorns and thistles. The curse, however, brought dramatic changes. It was an active judgement involving the exercise of God's mighty power. Thorns and thistles were brought into being, accompanying the other active judgements that affected the serpent (3:14) and the woman (3:16).

God's punishment of Cain
(Genesis 4:1-17)

EXPLANATION

Sin soon broke apart the bonds of family love. Cain was consumed by anger and jealousy, and he murdered his brother Abel. God said, 'Your brother's blood cries out to me from the ground' (v. 10). The punishment that came to him from God shows some similarities with the punishment pronounced upon Adam. It also is described as a curse (v. 11).

Cain was to be exiled ('driven from the ground', 'a restless wanderer on the earth', vv. 11-12). We should recall that Adam and Eve were previously banished from God's presence (3:23).

Cain's relationship with the ground was affected. It is worth noting that previously 'Cain worked the soil' (4:2), but now God declares: 'When you work the ground, it will no longer yield its crops for you' (v. 12). The ground was to be smitten by God, so that it would be barren and unproductive. Again, we should recall that Adam was promised a hard time working the ground: 'By the sweat of your brow you will eat your food' (3:19).

The case of Cain shows us not only that sin affects the way man exercises dominion over creation, but also that God is no passive observer. He is active in judgement and his punishments brought changes to the world he had created.

The wickedness leading to the Flood
(Genesis 6:1-22)

PRACTICAL TASKS

*Read Genesis chapter 6 and see if the same features
of God's judgements on man's sin are also prominent
in the most dramatic incident of judgement recorded in
Scripture: the great Flood in the time of Noah.*

1. What led to the LORD being 'grieved that he had made
   man on the earth' (v. 6)?

2. What explains God's decision to 'wipe mankind, whom
   I have created, from the face of the earth'?

3. What explains God's decision to 'destroy both them
   and the earth' (vv. 13, 17)?

In the cases of Adam, Cain and the people in the time of
Noah, God's judgements involved in different ways the
earth, the ground and the animals — even though the
sin was the responsibility of humans alone. What does
this tell us about the relationship between mankind and
the world around us?

The prophetic vision

EXPLANATION

Just as the theme of man's redemption is taken up in the prophetic writings of the Old Testament, so also is the theme of deliverance from the Edenic curse and other judgements affecting the ground. Instead of the thorn bush and the briers, redemption brings pine trees and the myrtle (Isaiah 55:13). God's purpose of redemption affects everything — so man's relationship with the created order must be affected. Isaiah 65:17-25 presents a vision of the new heavens and the new earth. The following verses offer particular allusions to deliverance from the Edenic curse.

verse 22: 'my chosen ones will long enjoy the works of their hands';

verse 23: 'They will not toil in vain';

verse 25: 'The wolf and the lamb will feed together, and the lion will eat straw like the ox.'

Verse 25 is particularly interesting, because we have a vision of an end of animals being carnivores and their return to eating plant food (Genesis 1:30 indicates that they were originally created as herbivores). If this understanding is correct, then there were many miraculous changes associated with the Edenic curse — all with the intention of bringing God's judgements to bear on man's dominion over creation.

Creation is to be redeemed

Perhaps the most significant commentary on these matters comes from Paul in Romans 8:18-25: 'The creation was subjected to frustration, not by its own choice.' The frustration was imposed because of Adam's sin. But one day, 'The creation itself will be liberated from its bondage to decay and brought into the glorious freedom of the children of God.' Then, the curse will be taken away. 'We know that the whole creation has been groaning in the pains of childbirth right up to the present time.' Creation today is not as it came from the hand of God! What we see today is abnormal.

After creation, our first parents met with God as he walked in the garden. This relationship was spoiled when Adam and Eve sinned and were cast out of Eden. Significantly, the terminology of God 'walking among his people' continues to be used in the Bible (Leviticus 26:12; 2 Corinthians 6:16). The redeemed people of God know something of what it was like to be in Eden!

The concept of redemption is normally applied to people. However, the very fact that it is applied also to creation is highly significant. It means that creation is not just suffering passively at the hands of mankind. Rather, creation has been cursed because of Adam's sin and is in a state of bondage. Creation needs to be redeemed. Just as the first Adam had dominion over creation (and Adam's sin led to the cursing of creation), so also the second Adam has dominion over creation (and Christ's work of redemption is good news for the whole cosmos). The Christian hope involves not only the transformation of people, but also the transformation of the fallen creation.

Paul's account of creation history can be summarized as follows:

1. *Created harmony*: very good, before the Edenic curse.
2. *A present-day state of frustration*: 'subjected to frustration'; in a state of 'bondage to decay'; 'groaning as in the pains of childbirth'.
3. *A state of future perfection*: 'liberated from its bondage and brought into the glorious freedom of the children of God'.

This timeline, with a few embellishments, is presented opposite in visual form.

Science applied to origins: is the present the key to the past?

Two types of science are worth distinguishing when the question of origins is considered. The first type looks for explanations about 'how things work' and the second asks questions about 'how things came to be'. The first requires laboratories and an experimental programme. The second requires the scientist to work as a detective, looking for clues that allow questions to be answered.

EXPLANATION

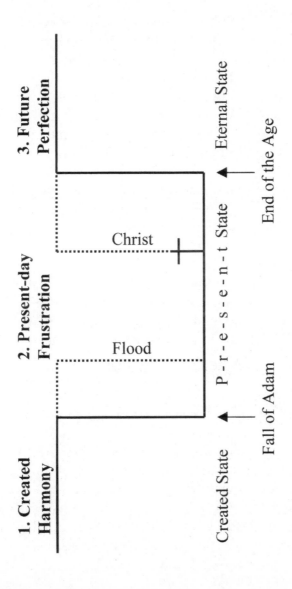

Three states of creation

The first type operates entirely within the present state of creation. We study how the creation works in its 'present-day frustration'. The second type is, however, frequently used to answer questions about ultimate origins. It is here that major areas of conflict are to be found, because many researchers deny that there was a state of created harmony. At the outset, then, there can be quite different perceptions about how science should approach such questions.

If the 'three states of creation' model is valid, then any attempt to make the present order of things 'normal' must be fundamentally flawed. In particular, the 'problem of pain' is only a problem in the present-day state of frustration. It was not known in the initial state of harmony, because sin and pain were absent. It will not be known in the perfected state, because sin will belong to the past and the mysteries of God's sovereignty will become a stimulus for worship.

We have here a major reason why Christians should not adopt Darwinism. The evolutionary approach to origins takes things that we see today and makes them the mechanisms of transformation. Today, we see the struggle for survival, death, decay and pain. We see the cycle of birth and death. With Darwin, we see variation and we see natural selection. But whereas we see the operation of the world under the Edenic curse, Darwin saw these things as the means of bringing the world of living things into existence.

Christians who adopt Darwinism appear to be unaware that the 'problem of pain' is embedded in their theory. Evolutionary explanations cannot avoid saying that pain, suffering and death are 'normal' and in no way connected to the sin of Adam. To evolutionists, the world that we see today is essentially the world that has always been. The present is the key to the past. There has been no Fall in history and no Edenic curse. If there is a Creator God, he must have made the world like this. This means evolutionists are making important theological statements about the world and, as a consequence, run headlong into the problem of pain. Some evolutionists see this clearly. If there is a god, they say, he must be held accountable — for he used pain, suffering and death as the means of bringing living things from simple cells to complex organisms. Blaming it on Adam, they say, before he was ever born, is an absurdity.

Our consideration of the original state of creation and the changes that occurred as a consequence of Adam's sin has led to us reviewing many of the teachings we find in Scripture. It has also led to us identifying reasons why the theory of evolution takes a theological position on the 'problem of pain' that is irreconcilable with Scripture.

QUESTIONS FOR DISCUSSION

DISCUSS IT

1. What does the Bible teach about the initial state of creation? Could the 'very good' affirmation that God gives in Genesis 1 be said of the world we live in today? If not, why not?

2. Genesis 3 is a controversial chapter, even among Christians. Some say it is history and others say it is written in some other literary style — but is not historical. Consider whether it matters what Christians believe. Explain what you believe about this chapter, and why, to another Christian.

3. How would you seek to help someone who was struggling with the 'problem of pain'?

4. The Bible encourages us to think positively about our future life with Christ. What changes will Christ bring at the end of the age? What changes will he bring to you; and to the world in which we live?

THE GUIDE

CHAPTER SEVEN

UNDERSTANDING GOD'S PURPOSE IN CREATION

BIBLE READING

Genesis 1

For perhaps thirty years, the Big Bang theory has dominated thinking about origins. It has been the account students learn in textbooks. It is the story that has been presented as fact by the media. Scientific research has sought to fill in the details. However, during the 1990s, a growing disquiet with the Big Bang was apparent, and finally, a few weeks before this chapter was written, a new cosmological theory of origins was published in the prestigious journal *Science*.

The new theory utilizes many concepts that are unfamiliar even to the educated layman. These include string theory, branes and eleven dimensions of space-time (instead of the four that we are used to). This is not the place to comment further on the model, except to point out that the new theory has no place for the beginning of time. Instead, we are presented with endless cycles of cause and effect. Universes come into existence, they evolve and then each one collapses and dies. We exist in one of these cycles. By chance, our universe has permitted the evolution of not only life but also intelligent life.

Many Christians saw the Big Bang as a theory of origins with which they were comfortable. They were happy that there was a beginning, because that is what the Bible teaches. They were happy to note that the universe appears to be eminently suited for life, because they could point to God as the designer. They were often quick to point out that the Bible is not a textbook of science, so we should not expect to find anything in it that cosmologists could use. However, if the new theory becomes widely accepted, this approach to harmonizing the Bible and origins begins to look very outdated. The new theory has no beginning to time, and the evidences for design are just superficial because the number of universes is very large and those that happen to have suitable conditions become homes for life.

Christians must beware of reading the Bible with the latest scientific thinking in mind. We need to read it as the Word of the ever-living God to us. As we saw in chapter 1 of this guide, although God spoke into cultures distant from ours, he did not speak in a way that makes understanding possible only for the scholar. In the Bible, God reveals what he wants ordinary people from all cultures to know about origins. Our goal must be to receive and respond to this revelation.

Genesis means 'beginnings' in Hebrew. Christians need never feel apologetic because we have teachings and beliefs about origins. Actually, it is fundamental

WORK AT IT

to our understanding of truth. Perhaps the first thing that we can say about beginnings is that God alone is eternal. He has no beginning, so it is meaningless to ask the question 'Who created God?' Secondly, we can say that there was a real beginning to the created order and to time. Both these truths come from the first verse of the Bible: 'In the beginning God created the heavens and the earth.'

Genesis 1 overview

PRACTICAL TASKS

Read Genesis chapter 1 and make a list of everything God made on each day. Your list should have the same level of detail as the text of Genesis 1.

In this chapter, we are considering some of the key teachings of Genesis chapter 1. It is a remarkable chapter and it never seems to weary those who give their attention to it. Here are none of the battling gods that appear in the creation accounts of other ancient human cultures. Rather, here we have the step-by-step creation of all material things by one who knows what he is doing. Unformed matter becomes a wonderful home for plants, animals and humanity.

At every stage, God is in control and almighty creative power accompanies his spoken words. Since God's power appears unlimited, he need not have created in six days. He could have spoken the word and everything would have appeared in an instant! It follows that the chronology recorded in this chapter is for our benefit and is in no way a reflection on God's ability. The question 'Why did God choose to create in six days?' is therefore entirely appropriate.

It has long been recognized that a very significant sequence of events is recorded in Genesis 1. There is a pattern of three days of 'forming' and three days of 'filling', followed by God's rest, as shown by the overview below.

Creation summary:	*Verse 1*: Overview of creation out of nothing
Forming:	*Verses 2-5*: light and darkness, day and night (day 1)
	Verses 6-8: sea (waters below) and sky (waters above — clouds) (day 2)
	Verses 9-13: land, plants (day 3)
Filling:	*Verses 14-19*: sun, moon and stars (day 4)
	Verses 20-23: sea creatures and birds (day 5)
	Verses 24-31: land animals and man (day 6)
Creation complete:	*2:1-3*: the rest of God (day 7)

EXPLANATION

On days 1-3, God *forms* his creation, transforming it from the 'formless' state (v. 2) to where it can support animal life on Earth. He forms the day and the night (day 1), the sea and sky (day 2), and the vegetated land (day 3). On days 4-6, God *fills* each domain he has made. The day has the sun and the night has the moon and stars. The sea has the sea creatures and the sky has the birds. The vegetated land has animals and man.

The chapter records a purposeful Creator, working systematically to prepare a place in which man, his image-bearer, can happily dwell. Designer people are placed on a designer Earth. Man is not just the last of God's creations, he is the most significant part of the created order. We have already noted the way God took counsel with himself when he came to create man. We have also recognized that man was given dominion over all the other animals. It appears as though the spotlight in Genesis 1 is on the creation of man, although we need also to give thought to the seventh day rest of God. This topic is considered further in chapter 12.

God could have created in an instant, but he did not. The real issue is not how long the days were — because the emphasis is on God's design (forming and filling) rather than the timescale. These things occurred for our benefit, not God's.

Nevertheless, since the book of Genesis is essentially historical, we should anticipate that a creation day is meaningfully related to the period of time we call a day.

The Earth: a prepared planet

The uniqueness of planet Earth is apparent even at a junior school level of appreciation of our solar system. The Gas Giant planets are too cold, too large and lack oxygen in their atmospheres. Life would be simultaneously frozen, crushed and asphyxiated! Of the inner planets, Mercury's temperatures are too extreme and there is no atmosphere. Venus is an oven and has a corrosive and deadly atmosphere. Mars' surface temperature can rise above the freezing point of water, but its atmosphere is very thin and is lacking in oxygen and water. The Moon is almost as inhospitable as Mercury — and the Apollo missions demonstrated that all life-support systems have to be carried by the visitors. There are no indigenous life forms.

Contrast all this with the Earth: the temperatures are suitable, the atmosphere is rich in oxygen and lacking harmful gases, there is a plentiful supply of liquid water, and the Earth's gravitational properties enable a wide range of living structures to be viable.

ILLUSTRATION

God created the Moon to 'govern the night', not to sustain life. When living things go to the Moon, they must take all their life-support systems with them.

(Image courtesy of NASA)

Despite these basic facts, there are many who question the uniqueness of the Earth. They argue that there must be millions of planets out there and, even if only a few happen to have suitable properties, there must still be vast numbers of planets like ours. The science-fiction writers have had a field day with these arguments, and this has helped to raise expectations with the public at large. Now that planets orbiting stars are being detected, the hype has increased further, despite the fact that none of these newly-discovered planets would be suitable to sustain life — they are typically too large or too hot.

Nevertheless, enthusiasts point to the fact that we are discovering planets out there — and these must be the tip of the iceberg! The response we make is to say that the features associated with the Earth's uniqueness are also being explored in greater detail. More and more pointers to the Earth being designed for life are being discovered. If the issue is to be decided by statistics, then planets suitable for the emergence of intelligent life are increasingly unlikely. Planet Earth is filled with life only because it has been formed (prepared) for this purpose.

Despite all this, the search for extraterrestrial life, and particularly for extraterrestrial intelligence (SETI) has been prominent in the media for over forty years and has involved the expenditure of large sums of money. The unceasing enthusiasm for continuing the quest, in the complete absence of any positive data, points to an agenda going beyond scientific inquisitiveness. Sometimes this is expressed openly: 'If only we can find life elsewhere, it will prove that life on Earth is not a miracle. Then we will know that life evolves naturally without the need to involve God.'

This is not the place to present the scientific issues, but the aim here is to start with a biblical foundation (the Earth as a prepared planet) and recognize that this can be harmonized with other knowledge coming from the sphere of science. The more we know from science about planet Earth, the less ordinary it appears.

DISCUSS IT

QUESTIONS FOR DISCUSSION

1. If the Bible teaches that time has a beginning, what can we say to scientists who build their theories on the thought that there is no beginning, only endless cycling? Read Genesis 1:1 and Hebrews 11:3. Do these verses have any bearing on cosmology? Is it fair to say that the Bible can inform scientists even if it does not attempt to be a scientific textbook?

2. Look again at your list of what happened on each day. Does the structure of 'forming' and 'filling' mean that Genesis 1 is not historical?

3. Every year, the media carries stories about the search for extraterrestrial life. Is there a Christian view on this? On statistical grounds, is 'forming' and 'filling' something that must happen many times in the universe?

4. Next time you hear a report about a new planet discovery, consider the following questions. How much of the report is science and how much is speculation? Is the emphasis on exploring the universe, or is it 'looking for evidence that we are not alone'? Are there spiritual issues here?

CHAPTER EIGHT

UNDERSTANDING GOD'S PURPOSE IN SEXUALITY, MARRIAGE AND THE FAMILY

LOOK IT UP

BIBLE READING

Genesis 2:18-25

INTRODUCTION

Young people today are growing up in a world that is characterized by transient, rather than permanent, relationships. Films and television dramas are full of marital unfaithfulness, heartbreak and the manipulation of people's emotions and trust. Magazines and books seem to win readers by engaging human interest in the traumas of romance, the experience of illicit sex, and the pain of losing a loved one to another.

The UK statistics make for grim reading. 50% of marriages are ended by divorce and 30% end within five years. About 40% of children are born outside marriage. Teenage pregnancies outside marriage are increasing. Many children now live in a single-parent home. As a result, social workers prefer to speak of 'parenting', rather than 'fathering and mothering' — because 'parenting' reduces feelings of exclusion. School books portraying more traditional family relationships are a 'cause for concern' to some, because so many children cannot relate to a father who loves and protects his children rather than someone who lives away from home and who generates fear rather than trust. 'Fathering' is not an acceptable word because, for many children, the father brings domestic violence. People are choosing to live together rather than make lifetime commitments within the framework of marriage. It is normal now to refer to someone's 'partner' rather than her 'husband' or his 'wife'.

People feel chained — but what happens when the chain is broken? Sad to say, many find the liberated life to be a new form of slavery.

In contemporary culture, there is a longing for relationships that are liberated from traditional moral codes. The search for freedom replaces the bondage of rules and regulations. Few approach the whole issue of sexuality by asking: 'What is God's plan for my life?' There is, as a result, a vacuum in people's thinking and this is filled by the values drawn from friends and films. The hunger for liberty and freedom in sexuality brings excitement and the expectation of fulfilment.

With the quest for liberation, words take on new meanings. 'Male' and 'female' terminology is banished to biology lessons and played down when it comes to developing human relationships. Even the word 'sex' has become unpopular in some circles, because it implies there are real differences. 'Gender' has replaced 'sex' in the language of many advocates of liberty.

Moreover, this revisionism comes with a new moral code. There is a cultural agenda that is hostile to biblical values. Many will talk at length about homosexual relationships, homosexual parents, single parents and heterosexual marriage relationships — but without reference to our Creator's commands.

PRACTICAL TASKS

Consider Jesus' teaching on marriage and the reference he made to Genesis chapters 1 and 2. Read Matthew 19:1-12 and Genesis 2:4-25.

- The Pharisees knew that the Law of Moses permitted divorce, but they were divided as to the grounds for divorce. How did Jesus respond to their question?
- Jesus' conclusion was: 'Therefore what God has joined together, let not man separate.' How does this conclusion follow from the verses quoted?

WORK AT IT

- From verse 8, how are we to understand the Mosaic Law that allowed divorce?
- What is the teaching of the Lord Jesus for those of his followers who marry?

Marriage as a covenant relationship

Genesis chapter 2 provides further information about the events of day 6. Adam and Eve were not created at exactly the same time. Adam was made first and he gave names to all the animals God had made (2:19-20). This served two purposes. First, it was a response to the command of God that mankind should rule over creation, because the 'naming' is carried out by someone in authority. Second, it meant that Adam had a good look at each kind of animal God had created, and he was able to see whether any of them could satisfy his need for companionship.

None of the animals were found to be a suitable 'helper' for Adam. Adam was 'alone' and this was not good (2:18). The animals could not converse with Adam; they could not provide the personal relationship he was capable of and hungered for; they lacked an aesthetic appreciation of the creation and they were not creative. In other words, they were not image-bearers and they could not provide the companionship, support and partnership that Adam needed.

So God created woman. Genesis 1 gives the overview: both male and female are image-bearers, both are commanded to be fruitful and increase in number, both are given the command to subdue the Earth and to rule. In Genesis 2, more details are given. God gave Adam a wife by bringing her to him (v. 22). God made the relationship, although Adam was a very willing participant (see v. 23). His response shows a sense of exhilaration in the provision of such a delightful helper.

What is the nature of this God-made relationship? Was it transient or permanent? Was it to last as long as Adam and Eve felt good about it, but dispensable if not? The answer must be no. If God makes the relationship, he must have the right to end it. To express this clearly, Christians have described marriage as a 'covenant' relationship. A covenant creates a bonded, permanent relationship between two parties. The relationship between Adam and Eve was not one of 'we choose to live together'. By contrast, contemporary marriage is reduced to a contract that is often no more than a bill of sale.

Human sexuality

God created both man and woman, male and female. Sexual distinctions are part of the created order. The differences are not superficial, as though they can be negated by cultural factors, social pressures and, more recently, by the surgeon's knife. People have not invented sexual differences! They are a matter of creation.

Consequently, our first response to human sexuality should be to give thanks to God for making us this way.

God commanded our first parents to have children and to fill the Earth. Sexual relations within marriage are thus part of the created order. Since God declares the results of the sixth day as 'very good', we can safely include sexuality within the list of things that God delights in. Those religious traditions that treat sex as 'earthly' and hostile to spirituality have not gained their teachings from Genesis 1! Nor is it apparent in the Song of Songs, the book of the Bible that uses the full range of emotions and feelings drawn from the marriage relationship to teach spiritual truths.

I was a teenager during the 1960s, when there were very strong views expressed about liberating young people from inhibiting moral traditions. There was much talk of Victorian values that once repressed human sexuality. The older generation was mocked because it was not able to speak freely about sex. A generation has passed, and my own view is that the libertarians and advocates of sexual freedom are now in a far worse state than their parents! People want to talk freely about sexuality, but they do not know how to do it without demeaning the opposite sex, or without indulging in depraved humour. Innumerable people cannot handle sex at all, and they resort to pornography and self-abuse. They are the victims of various forms of sexual exploitation managed by the booming sex industry, carefully feeding reassurances about liberty and freedom to the enslaved.

My own experience is that only a well-grounded belief in creation gives men and women, young and old, the intellectual, moral and spiritual resources to handle sex wisely. The will to say 'no' to sexual temptation and to extra-marital sex can crumble before peer group pressure. However, when our peer group is the Lord God himself, we have an anchor in the storm that delivers us from making a shipwreck of our lives.

The marriage partnership and roles

Both male and female were commissioned to rule and to subdue the Earth. Insofar as ruling and having dominion is a shared responsibility, women are no less image-bearers than men. God treated our first parents as partners. In many cultures, the situation is quite different. Women are not expected to have any responsibilities apart from child-rearing, and the result is cultural and social impoverishment. Not only do those societies lose the input that women can make, but also male/female relationships are adversely affected because gender differences are not understood in the light of partnership before God.

We must also note that Adam was created first. The context for the creation of woman was Adam's need for companionship and help (Genesis 2:18).

As far as their humanity is concerned, men and women are equal, but within the marriage relationship they have different functions and responsibilities. The marriage relationship is essentially a two-person team, with husband and wife being complementary to one another. Within marriage, the husband represents both partners and carries the responsibility for both. Thus, although the woman was first in the transgression, it was 'in Adam' that we sinned (Romans 5:12-17). The fact that Adam was created first is part of the argument of the apostle Paul in 1 Timothy 2:13.

Of course, the created order has been affected by sin. As we have already seen from Matthew 19, provision was made for divorce under the Mosaic Law, because of the hardness of heart of the people. We can see a change in the 'partnership' relationship immediately after the entrance of sin in Eden. Adam had already named the animals, exercising his authority and rule over creation. Significantly, he did not name his wife before their act of disobedience. However, after the Fall, Adam named his wife 'Eve' (Genesis 3:20). By doing this, he was asserting authority over his partner. Instead of a partnership of equals, his marriage became a relationship with Adam as ruler and Eve as ruled. But, using the words of the Lord Jesus in Matthew 19:8: 'It was not this way from the beginning.'

There is much more teaching in the Bible, particularly in the New Testament, about marriage, sexuality and the roles of husbands and wives. We have seen that the foundations for these teachings are to be found in the first three chapters of Genesis. Everyone reading these words is either facing or will soon need to face some of these issues, and this means building on the foundation. All the more reason to make sure the foundation is secure!

QUESTIONS FOR DISCUSSION

DISCUSS IT

1. Pets provide some companionship, but can they provide the deeper relationship that marriage brings? Identify relevant verses of Scripture and discuss similarities and differences.

2. How should married couples set out to develop the relationship that God has intended? Discuss possible ways of expressing partnership between two image-bearers who are both charged with ruling (forming) and filling the earth (Genesis 1:26)?

3. Read Ephesians 5:21-33. How does this passage handle the themes of partnership, companionship, leadership and covenant? What is the meaning of verse 31, which quotes Genesis 2:24?

4. What are the implications of these teachings for single people? You should revisit Matthew 19:10-12 when considering how a Christian should approach singleness.

CHAPTER NINE

'LET THERE BE LIGHT ... AND LIVING THINGS'

BIBLE READING

Psalm 104

Like most parents, my wife and I have very precious memories of the first words of our children. The transition from baby noises to baby speaking is sheer delight. In many ways, it does not matter what the child says, the fact that a word is spoken is sufficient to stir the heart! First words, and first impressions, are also very important in adult life. Some friends have the amazing ability to learn more about someone from a short introduction than I am able to learn from many meetings! Nothing, however, can compare with God's introduction and the first words that are recorded in the Bible: 'Let there be light' (Genesis 1:3). What makes this so striking is that as a result of God speaking, there was light!

What is the link between God's words, the creation of light, and true history? This chapter is about the relationship between the commands of God in Genesis 1 and the consequences. Are we in the realm of miracles or are we in the realm of the natural? And how do we relate these things to the origin of animals and plants?

Creation and providence revisited

Genesis 1 records God speaking many words of command. The Earth was formed and filled according to the commands of its Creator. According to the Bible, we cannot understand origins unless we see God as the central figure. The universe did not just happen, as though God were irrelevant to the whole process. Furthermore, we are to understand that God's speaking was a matter of personal choice. His hand was not forced. The universe did not have to come into existence, and the Earth did not have to be like it is. God is not like the deist's god who created the universe in the Big Bang and then let things run their course — as a self-assembling system (even if that were possible).

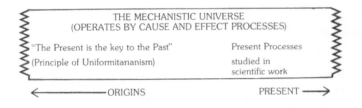

The mechanistic science of deists and other evolutionists
(with no beginning and no end of time).

Psalm 33:9 says, 'For he spoke, and it came to be; he commanded, and it stood firm.' Are we to understand in this text an allusion to God's speaking in Creation Week? In particular, we need to ask whether God's creative word is a clear pointer to miracle or whether

EXPLANATION

we should understand that God was using processes (which we can comprehend) to bring living things into existence.

The Scriptures repeatedly teach God's sovereignty over all things. He upholds all things: he makes the sun shine, the rain fall and the grass grow (Psalm 104). We glory in the way he cares for his creatures. We recognize God's hand in processes we call 'natural'. Paul proclaimed to the people of Athens: 'For in him we live and move and have our being' (Acts 17:28). Natural processes are natural because this is God's normal way of exercising control over creation. The Scriptures witness to Christ, who is 'sustaining all things by his powerful word' (Hebrews 1:3). Were these natural processes the means God used to create?

Before we answer these questions, we need to remind ourselves that God is in no sense confined to this 'natural' way of working. God is intimately involved with his creation and he does what he wills. He is not limited by the laws of physics and chemistry — for he made these laws! He is able to make iron float (2 Kings 6:6). He can make it possible for people to enter a fiery furnace without even being singed (Daniel 3:26-27). He can stop the mouths of hungry lions (Daniel 6:21). He can make the sun's shadow go back on a sundial (2 Kings 20:9-11). He can make the sun stay in the middle of the sky for a full day

(Joshua 10:12-14). He is able to make a special star appear in the sky (Matthew 2:9). These examples point to God's supernatural ways of working that we call miracles.

So how are we to understand God's speaking in Creation Week? We have seen in chapter 2 that the distinction between creation and providence in Scripture is not fuzzy. Creation is a finished activity and is spoken of in the past tense. Providence is ongoing, and is described as upholding that which has been created. To suggest that creation was accomplished using providential processes is to confuse these distinct categories of thought. Of course, there is much more that can be said. Creation involves intelligent design. It involves new information. The Scriptures do not link these characteristics with the workings of providence.

CREATION (MIRACLE)	PROVIDENCE (UPHOLDING AND ORDERING OF CREATION)
Cannot be studied	May be studied — scientific work
ORIGINS (CREATION WEEK)	PRESENT (ALL TIME SINCE CREATION WEEK)

The framework for science as perceived by biblical theists (with a clear beginning and end of time).

Consequently, we conclude that the creative words of God in Genesis 1 are intended to convey the meaning of God's miraculous activity. Psalm 33:9 can properly be understood as referring to a miracle.

PRACTICAL TASKS

The Lordship of Jesus over creation

We know that the miracles of Christ were 'signs' (John 2:11). The question is, what did they signify? Consider the following miracles and write down what should have been learned by those who witnessed these mighty works.

- Changing the water into wine (John 2:1-11)
- Stilling the storm (Mark 4:35-41)
- Walking on the water (Matthew 14:22-32)
- Innumerable cases of healing the sick
- Three cases of him raising the dead

After Jesus healed the deaf and mute man (Mark 7:31-37), the people were overwhelmed with amazement. They exclaimed: 'He has done everything well.' These words are remarkably close to those found in the Septuagint (Greek) version of Genesis 1:31, where God saw all that he had made and it was 'very good'. We should learn from this that the people (or at least Mark) recognized a link between the miraculous works of Christ in healing and the miraculous works of God in creation.

A New Testament guide to the meaning of the words 'Let there be light' (Genesis 1:3) comes from one of Paul's letters. 'For God, who said,

"Let light shine out of darkness", made his light shine
in our hearts to give us the light of the knowledge of
the glory of God in the face of Christ' (2 Corinthians
4:6). The context for these words is the new birth, the
miraculous work of God in people's lives. Paul has in
mind something that sounds more like creation than
providence.

Miracles and origins

By contrast, evolutionary theory is strictly non-
miraculous. According to this theory, everything in the
past is governed by either natural law or chance. So, if
the Earth was in fact formed and filled miraculously,
we need to reject evolutionary accounts of the origins
of plants, fish, birds and land animals. In non-technical
language Paul writes: 'All flesh is not the same: Men
have one kind of flesh, animals have another, birds
another and fish another' (1 Corinthians 15:39). If creation was miraculous, there have been different 'kinds'
existing since creation, with the plain implication that
all flesh cannot be the same.

Darwinism traces all living things back to a common
ancestor. For this theory to work, there must be a complete continuity between all life forms. Evolutionists
create family trees that always go back to a single cell.
This approach is found in Darwin's *Origin of Species*
and is apparent in the only illustration he included in
his book.

EXPLANATION

The word 'kind' crops up repeatedly in Genesis 1 and in other parts of the Scriptures. The word reinforces the notion that the living world is made up of different biological groupings not connected by ancestors. Using scientific terminology, we might say that living things are distinguished by *discontinuities* between created groups. This approach conflicts with evolutionary theory, which requires continuity back to a common ancestor. To do justice to the discontinuities, creation-orientated biologists have developed technical terminology to complement the popular term, 'the Genesis kinds'.

The Genesis 'kinds'

Historically, there have been problems with the concept of the Genesis kinds. This is partly because in the Latin Bible, the Hebrew word for 'kind' was translated as 'species'. Christians in the past appeared to be unduly influenced by this. The creationist biologist and pioneer classifier of animals and plants, Carl Linnaeus, started his classification work by thinking that every species was as it came from the hand of God. Later, he realized that this could not be and that new species were not impossible or even unusual.

Creation-oriented biologists today understand many of the variations to result from design. It is important for the genetic health of organisms that variations occur, and it is also important for survival. Since environments change, organisms that have little or no capacity to adjust become extinct. The picture emerging is one of many created ancestors, each with a capacity for variation leading to speciation.

A good starting point for understanding variation is our own species. We use the terms 'mankind' and 'humankind', signifying an underlying belief that all humanity belongs to the same created kind. Yet we cannot avoid noticing the variations! The different races of man show differences in skin colour, hair texture, and many variations in bone shape.

The major races of mankind show different traits, but we are all descended from Adam and Eve (Mongoloid, Australoid, Negroid, Caucasian).

EXPLANATION

It hardly needs to be noted that people in Darwin's day were well aware of these variable characters and yet understood the Christian teaching that all were descended from Adam and Eve, our common ancestors. Variation within the created kind should not have been a difficult concept for Darwin to grasp. However, in his book, Darwin repeatedly interprets every example of variation as evidence *for* his theory and evidence *against* creation.

Against this we argue that evidences of variation are not evidences for a universal common ancestor. The data fits equally well into an understanding of biology where there are multiple ancestors. This is a topic we return to in chapter 13.

Why do so many find the 'evidences for evolution' overwhelming?

Daily we are exposed to media reports, commentaries and literature that takes 'the fact' of evolution for granted. At the time of writing, *Scientific American* is running a feature, written by the editor, with the title: '15 Answers to Creationist Nonsense'. The subtitle is: 'Opponents of evolution want to make a place for creationism by tearing down real science, but their arguments don't hold up'. Material like this can be an enormous burden for Christians. Who wants to be associated with 'nonsense'? Who wants to 'tear down real science'? Many Christians who know there is something wrong with this will have little background in science and cannot be expected to have a grasp of all the technical issues. How do we develop a response?

Our basic position should be one of opening minds to the data and to the debate. Evolutionists try hard to make it appear that people who believe what the Bible says about origins are bigoted and ignorant of the evidence. In this, they go back to the strategy adopted by Charles Darwin in his classic book, *On the Origin of Species*. Darwin portrayed the permanence of species as the only position adopted by creationists. Then, any evidence for speciation was treated as evidence for his theory. This was a 'straw man' argument — but something like this was needed to make his points convincing. The same strategy continues to this day, because Darwinists seem unable to admit that evidence for variation and speciation are readily understood within a creationist framework. Opening minds means helping people to see where their arguments are falsely constructed and approaching data with a mind that is not already made up.

Christians must practise what we preach. We need never have fears about this counsel of openness because God is the author of all truth. Since he is the truth, all tensions between revealed truth and the study of the natural world are only apparent. In my experience, tensions can usually be traced back to our limited knowledge of either the science or the Scriptures. 'Those who seek shall find' applies not just to the Kingdom of Heaven, but also to the practice of science. It does matter, however, with what spirit we act. God calls us to a prayerful, humble and diligent seeking in whatever we do.

QUESTIONS FOR DISCUSSION

DISCUSS IT

1. Are there any differences between God's miraculous works and his normal way of upholding his creation? Identify some Bible verses that are relevant and discuss whether it is important for us to make a distinction.

2. Read John 1:1-4 and discuss the meaning of the phrase, 'Through him [the Word] all things were made'. When 'the Word' speaks, what happens?

3. What does it mean for a Christian to have an 'open mind'? Consider this by referring to John 1:9 and 2 Corinthians 4:1-6. (These verses have direct relevance to knowing God and entering into his truth, but does this mean questions about origins are excluded?) What can you do to help yourself develop an open mind?

4. *How closely do the Scriptures define the Genesis 'kinds'? Read Genesis 1 and Leviticus 11 and list the categories that are said to reproduce after their kind. Ask the question: does the Bible have species in mind, or does the text suggest groupings broader than species?*

CHAPTER TEN

LABOUR AND THE WORK ETHIC

BIBLE READING

Ecclesiastes 2:17-26

It might be considered surprising that a guide on creation addresses the issue of work. What has work to do with origins? The reason, in brief, is that a Christian understanding of work emphasizes that God has a *purpose* in our working, and his will is made clear in the early chapters of Genesis. Unless we ground our thinking in creation and the purpose of God, the reasons for working tend to revolve around its survival value and whatever other (personal) justification we want to give to it (e. g. to gain wealth). In too many cases, work fails to satisfy or bring any sense of fulfilment.

In the news at the time of writing is the problem of having only a small proportion of working-class young people experiencing higher education. The proportion of this social group going to university has hardly changed over twenty years, despite the great expansion in student numbers. This cannot be because working-class children are inherently less able

Many people think of work as an endless tread-mill.
'It gets us nowhere and certainly does not satisfy!'

(Image source: http://www.vegan-straight-edge.org.uk/work.htm)

to use their brains, so the conclusion has been drawn
that their educational attainments come far short of
their true potential. Not a few experts have been heard
to say that the education system has failed these young
people. Whatever may be the truth of this view, the
educational system is only part of the story. We need to
ask questions about the attitudes to work of young

people, from whatever social class they come. What affects their 'work ethic'? What motivates them to acquire skills to make them employable? These are pressing questions, and my goal in this chapter is to show that the Bible has full and satisfying answers for people of all social classes.

Work and image-bearing

God is a worker (Genesis 1). Genesis 2:2 refers to the 'work of creating' that he had done. Although that particular work is completed, God still works to provide for his creatures and to bring salvation. Jesus said, 'My Father is always at his work to this very day, and I, too, am working' (John 5:17). It follows that if God works, then work is worth doing. As we work, we are imitating God. This is a consequence of image-bearing. It is also a key element for Christian thinking about the nature of work.

Ruling over the created order (Genesis 1:26) and subduing it (1:28) are important issues for man as an image-bearer. They are also very significant for understanding the relationship between man and the world in which God has placed us. God's dominion is original; man's dominion is modelled after it but it is also an extension. As we have seen, God's work was to form and fill the Earth to be a fit place for humans

EXPLANATION

to dwell. In Genesis 1:26, we have the same elements but applied to mankind: forming our environment (by ruling and subduing) and filling it (by reproducing). God commands and authorizes man to do what he has done. However, man's work starts where God left off. God created our first parents and our work of forming and filling relates to the increase of the human population. Our task is to use all the gifts that God has bestowed on us to make this world a place that is fit for man to dwell in, together with the rest of God's creatures.

The main problems with work are associated with sin. Creation now bears the marks of the curse. God said to Adam, 'By the sweat of your brow you will eat your food' (Genesis 3:19). Work became toil, and this affects every activity in which man is engaged. Furthermore, the workers are themselves sinful and bring a complete range of problems leading to frustration, boredom and feelings of meaninglessness. Without an understanding of the effects of sin, we are liable to be confused about work. We need to appreciate that God commands us to work even though the world is fallen and we are sinful. As individuals, each of us has a personal calling to work in this present world.

Aspirations about our lives

It is natural for humans to think about the future. We all have ambitions at some stage of our lives. Children

EXPLANATION

have aspirations. Teenagers are often very conscious of the way educational choices affect career options. They dream dreams. Adults may still dream, but very often decisions are overtaken by events, or decisions are made for us. It is useful to reflect on why only humans have these concerns. Pets do not puzzle over what they will do when they grow up. Wild animals do not grapple with deep questions about the meaning of life! They do not — because they are not made in the image of God.

What does God call us to do in life? Which people influence us so that we want to be like them? Who are our role models? Those who have a calling to be preachers and missionaries have no shortage of inspiring resources to encourage, to instruct and to envision. However, what about the rest of us who are not called to these ministries? How do we recognize God's calling for us? How do we develop a vocation? Unless we have a clear idea on this, we shall end up with media figures as role models. This is the way of the world and it appears to be a real danger for Christian young people. We only have to look at the vast sums of money passing over in sponsorship deals and in advertising to realize that media figures (in sport and in entertainment) have a tremendous influence over our youth. But are these people portraying a lifestyle that brings us closer to God?

Does it matter what we do as long as we are witnesses for Jesus? The danger in thinking like this is also thinking that God is not calling us to the work or role we are doing. 'Tentmaking' is often the word used to mean any work that allows us to earn sufficient money to do the things that really matter! Paul did not practise 'tentmaking' in this way! He was a tentmaker — that was his trade (Acts 18:3). However, he was never disparaging about this aspect of his life. He was willing to earn money by practising his trade so that he would not be a financial burden to others.

Similarly, our vocation is an essential part of our witness to the Lord. Our starting point for recognizing God's call on our lives is Genesis 1:28. Image-bearers are called to exercise 'rule'. We are called to 'subdue' the Earth. The Royal Law is not only to be ruling in us, but also through us. To exercise dominion is to transform our surroundings — to the glory of God.

Seeing our work through God's eyes

- Read Nehemiah chapters 1-2. Nehemiah was a godly Jew in a foreign land. He was working as the royal cupbearer, which means that he had the full trust and confidence of the king. What can we learn from these chapters about God's purpose in Nehemiah's work? What was Nehemiah's attitude to his work? In what ways was he able to 'subdue' the Earth?

- Read 2 Kings chapter 5. We do not even know the name of the young girl who became the slave of Naaman's wife, but she is a key figure in this story. What was God's purpose in her being a slave? Can we learn anything about her attitude to her work? Although a slave, was she able to respond in any way to God's command to 'rule' (Genesis 1:26)?

Subduing the Earth

Paul reminded the Galatian Christians that they did not have the status of slaves in God's kingdom, but the status of sons. Christ came that we might receive the 'full rights of sons' (Galatians 4:5) and live as heirs. As sons and daughters of God, our calling is to subdue the Earth, and to exercise 'rule' in the name of the Lord Jesus Christ. This is true whatever our social class and whatever community we belong to.

These principles apply to all areas of life. It does not matter whether our energies are spent in manual work or in scholarly work, whether we are looking after the family at home, whether we are at school, or whether we are retired from the world of work. Our lives need never be without direction. The dominion we exercise depends entirely on the vocation we have. An office cleaner will work this out quite differently from an office manager. Christ is our example here. How would he have exercised 'rule' if he had been in our situation?

How do we practise 'dominion'?

In the comments above, the 'dominion' emphasis leads to a positive and active lifestyle. As God's children, we are always looking for ways to express our calling to be image-bearers. Our working lives provide us with many opportunities. Other people see us and take note of what kind of people we are. As we obey God's call, we cannot help but be witnesses to Jesus Christ through our actions. Our prayer is that, alongside our actions, we shall grasp the opportunities to bear witness in word also.

We do not need to stop dreaming dreams. Many young people want to change the world — and that is exactly what God calls us to do by emulating his work of forming and filling. The task is affected by human rebellion against God and the way everything has been marred by sin. Consequently, our calling to work, to make this Earth a fit place to inhabit, complements our calling to be witnesses for Christ and to spread the good news of salvation. Both of these callings involve doing the works that God has purposed for us.

Before bringing this chapter to an end, it is worth noting that evolutionary thinking has been used to justify all sorts of ideas about the human experience.

EXPLANATION

Reference is often made to the Stone Age men who are said to be our ancestors. They had a hunter/gatherer existence and this lifestyle is said to be 'original' for humans. This is what is deemed to be 'natural' for us — hunting, pillaging and being aggressive. Using the same logic, some advocate a 'Palaeolithic diet', consuming only those foods that were likely to have been eaten by our supposed ancestors.

Furthermore, using the reasoning of evolutionists, the concept of the 'survival of the fittest' has been used to justify all sorts of practices, including the way we work and the way we do business. There is a problem with this. If we look hard enough, we can find the whole range of possibilities out there in the living world. Consequently, to take any one practice and apply that to human society is really quite arbitrary. It reduces to an exercise in subjective judgement. This is a long-standing problem with evolutionary ethics.

No Christian perspective on work is complete without an emphasis on caring rule, so that the world is a better place for all. It would be good if people were more aware of the lives of Christians who have worked through these principles in their own lives. The church fellowship gathering would be ideal for this, drawing on the experiences and testimonies of members.

QUESTIONS FOR DISCUSSION

1. *For some, the ideas in this chapter will be new. You have learned about 'work' from others but have not realized that the Bible has much to say about it. Consider particularly the purpose of God for man to 'rule' (Genesis 1:26), and consider also the way sin has affected our task of ruling (Genesis 3:19). How do these thoughts change the way you think about work?*

2. *Why did Paul make tents when he was in Corinth (Acts 18:3)? Was he doing something he would later regret? Or was he teaching by example?*

3. *Imagine you are in a church fellowship meeting, and you are invited to explain to the young people present how your work relates to God's command to rule over and subdue the Earth. What would you say?*

4. *How is God's command for us to 'rule' compatible with our being 'strangers and aliens' in the world? Read Psalm 8 and Hebrews 2:5-9.*

CHAPTER ELEVEN

CREATION AND THE ENVIRONMENT

BIBLE READING

Genesis 1:26-30

INTRODUCTION

Many environmentalists think that Christianity has been a disaster for conservation. They think that the command to 'subdue the Earth' is bad news: a warrant for exploitation. They think that people who have exercised 'rule' over animals in times past have been self-serving and are responsible for our present environmental crisis. Consequently, Christians are accused of wanton desecration of the world and its various life forms.

Furthermore, environmentalism is not what it used to be! Animal rights are now very high on the agenda. In the United States, a new organization has been set up to provide legal representations for chimpanzees. The Chimpanzee Collaboratory bases its argument on genetics. Chimpanzees are 98.7% human in their genetic make-up, so why should they be denied rights? Steven Wise, a lawyer from the Center for the Expansion of Fundamental Rights, succeeded in getting a letter published in the prestigious science journal *Nature* (25 April 2002). He wrote: 'I say that a minimum level of autonomy — the abilities to desire, to act intentionally and to have some sense of self, whatever the species — is sufficient to justify the basic legal right to bodily integrity.' He pointed out: 'Such immunity rights as bodily integrity and freedom from slavery can belong to human children, infants, the very retarded, the profoundly senile and the insane.' Consequently, he went on, why not extend them to chimpanzees?

Chimpanzees have many skills. Some argue they should have the same legal rights as children.

We live in a society where many people are prepared to put themselves out for the sake of the environment. Typical activities are supporting pressure groups, participating in protests, writing letters, and boycotting

EXPLANATION

products from companies that are deemed to be exploiting the environment. People are also adopting 'green lifestyles' (recycling materials, going 'organic' and trying to put back into the environment as much as we take out of it). 'Environmentalism' is one of the key words of our generation.

Christians have not found it easy to work harmoniously with pressure group environmentalists. There are some valid reasons for this. Many in the green movements treat the world around us as sacred and regard human beings as parasites. This is not a Christian perspective. We are not pantheists (we do not believe that 'Nature is God'). Furthermore, we are called to 'subdue the Earth' (Genesis 1:28) and we are not willing to be described as parasites for doing this. Not all environmentalists, of course, think that humans are a scourge, but they do expect a positive agenda for the world around us and that animals and humans should coexist far better than we do at present.

Dominion: good and bad

Dominion means different things to different people. Many environmentalists regard it as a recipe for exploitation, to be avoided at all costs. Those who know the Lord recognize that the dominion God has ordained is patterned on Christ's dominion. He is the one of whom it is written: 'In putting everything under him, God left nothing that is not subject to him' (Hebrews 2:8). The Lord Jesus identifies himself as 'the ruler of God's creation' (Revelation 3:14). We have no warrant to do anything that the Lord Jesus Christ would not do. This is our standard and it means there can be no justification for Christians endorsing exploitation and environmental destruction.

That God calls us to care for the environment is also apparent from the creation account in the Bible. The Lord God took Adam and put him in the Garden of Eden 'to work it and take care of it' (Genesis 2:15). We have seen in chapter 10 of this guide that there is a distinctively Christian approach to work and that work is primarily a response of obedience to God. There is a harmonious continuity between the Christian teaching on work and the Christian teaching on the environment.

However, we must acknowledge that the biblical teaching has been abused. This sad situation should not surprise us. Wherever Christianity becomes a major influence in a community, there will be some who try to manipulate events to achieve their selfish ambitions. Not everyone living in a so-called Christian country is a Christian. It is not rare to find that people use biblical terminology for unworthy purposes. They justify exploitation of the world around us by appealing to their 'rights' of exercising dominion. Our responsibility is to challenge the abuse as well as to show what dominion really means.

Christian environmentalism

EXPLANATION

It is surely reasonable to point out that the 'Harvest Festival' service of thanksgiving to God is an affirmation of Christian environmentalism. We see our responsibilities to tend the land, and we give thanks to God when he gives the increase and blesses us with crops and fruit. Things have become more formal with fewer and fewer members of congregations having any experience of agriculture and even less knowing what it is to gain a harvest by the 'sweat of your brow'.

Some Christians today appear to have rediscovered the idea of environmental stewardship and there is a growing awareness of the issues. However, we have often given the impression that this is a low priority because few adopt a lifestyle in keeping with caring for the environment.

There is the additional problem that Christians have found little common ground with many active environmentalists. As noted earlier, we do not regard the world as especially sacred and we are certainly not pantheistic. We do not put animal life on a par with human life (let alone superior to it!). We do not regard our care for the environment as a substitute for discipleship, practical obedience and ministering to the needs of fellow humans.

Finding the right balance is not easy. Since most people today live in towns and cities, contact with the environment is more likely to come through television, books and holidays. There seems to be very little that we can actually do — apart from giving money to conservation projects. This perception, however, is not accurate. There are many ways we can respond to God's command to 'rule the Earth'.

To expand on this further, we must reflect first on the move of population from the land to the city. What social changes have taken place? The biggest transformation relates to the nature of work. People who live in farming communities tend to have many skills. Farming has always been dominant in my own family circle — on my mother's side. It has always impressed me how versatile these relatives have been. They have experience of all aspects of working with the land, but also in dealing with buildings, machinery and in running businesses. In many ways, these relatives have been self-sufficient and sharing resources within the community is just as important as purchasing products and services from others. By contrast, once people have moved into cities, their range of skills tends to diminish. Labour becomes very specialized. People train to do specific tasks, or study to become experts, in order to get jobs. The money they earn is needed to purchase all the things they themselves cannot provide.

Since city people are so involved in buying services and products, then this must be important for us as we look for ways of exercising environmental responsibility. Does it matter to us whether the Earth has been polluted or habitats destroyed in order to bring us

EXPLANATION

consumer goods? Do we seek out suppliers that are committed to sustainable trade? Basically, we need to cultivate a questioning attitude about environmental practices when we make purchases. What we cannot do ourselves, in terms of environmental responsibility, our suppliers can do. We should encourage them to provide an environmental policy that goes beyond compliance with legal requirements and actively seeks to make this world a better place for all living things.

Clearly, there are limitations to what can be achieved when the goods are consumer products. If few ask these questions, the supplier is unlikely to respond. The evidence appears to suggest that in the Western World taken as a whole, consumer expectations of environmental good practice are quite low. Fair Trade products, for example, rarely feature large in the shelves of supermarkets. Consequently, with few exceptions, the suppliers' codes of environmental practice do not go much beyond conformance to regulations. However, do not give up! Keep looking for suppliers who are more responsive to your particular interests. Make sure you 'put your money where your mouth is' when you do have a choice of supplier.

This is, of course, just a beginning. We need to think about lifestyle issues, the way we respond to advertising and packaging, the way we dispose of waste, and the way we develop our democratic rights as citizens. We cannot cover all these issues here. However, some pointers to ways of taking these principles further are given in this chapter's activity.

What is a Christian lifestyle?

Look at the 'lifestyle' passages below with the thoughts of this chapter in mind. Should it be possible to distinguish between sacrificial living as a disciple of the Lord Jesus and the radical lifestyle of a Christian environmentalist?

- *Matthew 6:28-33 and fine clothes.* Knowing that God takes pleasure in beauty, colour and aesthetics, should we also attend to the way we look and the way we dress? What can we learn from the way God clothes the lilies of the field? What is it to 'run after all these things' (v. 32)?

- *Luke 12:13-21 and the way we look upon our possessions.* What are our goals in life? How do we react when people tell us that a man's life consists in the abundance of his possessions? What is it to be 'rich towards God'?

• *James 4:13-17 and the busyness of life.* What motivation is James drawing attention to? What is lacking? How do we find out the good we ought to do?

As time passes, there are new challenges and new opportunities. We need to ask: 'What is God calling us to do in our own generation?'

Restoring a place for humanity within environmentalism

EXPLANATION

This chapter started by drawing attention to the increasing influence of animal rights activists. If evolution is true, their position is logical and defensible. There can be no clear line between the rights of humanity and the rights of the rest of the living world.

The Christian environmentalist has a robust explanation for the sanctity of human life and for mankind's place in the world. We are not guilty of stealing land from the animals, although we can be charged with stealing it from our Creator. God has made us stewards of land and sea and it is our responsibility to manage all for the benefit of both mankind and animals.

Not only does the world face environmental exploitation in the name of economic development and investor profits, it also suffers from the exploitation of humans. The problem is not

Christian environmentalism incorporates people and affects lifestyles

global trade, which brings many benefits to developing countries, but the abuse of economic power. Companies seek out the lowest cost of production and their sourcing strategy has the effect of driving down wages and increasing poverty. At its worst, it results in economic slavery.

The problems are largely hidden because consumers in developed countries like bargains. When we see a product that beats the competition on price, other issues (ethical sourcing and environmental good practice) hardly receive consideration. Initiatives that have been built on fair wages for producers are not well supported by the public.

Christian consumers ought to be among the most informed of the population about these issues. We owe it to these fellow men and women who make products for us. How can we read Christ's words about giving to the poor (Matthew 19:21) and then give our money to traders whose products are made by people who are paid less than the national minimum wage of their own country?

Dominion and stewardship

'Dominion' is a strong word, and most people have negative associations of 'dominion' (lording it over others). Consequently, there has been a tendency among Christians to speak almost exclusively of 'stewardship'. True, we are stewards under God, and what we do as stewards should be our response to his command. Clearly, there is no objection to this as far as it goes. There are plenty of biblical passages that develop the stewardship theme. However, we need to guard against the danger of weakening our sense of calling to rule as an aspect of image-bearing. Stewards can easily become passive, waiting for their master to initiate things. That is not the character that God would have us nurture.

Passivity as far as society is concerned is a recurrent theme in church history. This is perfectly understandable in times of persecution, but it has, unfortunately, been very influential at other times. Christians seem to think that they can only wait until the Lord comes again, as society is doomed.

The point to be made here is that this kind of passive Christianity tends to be weak in its teaching about creation. The vision is dim about the relationship Christians should have to the world that God has made. In particular, the command to 'rule over the Earth' is almost lost from view. Consequently, there has been an unhealthy distinction between things spiritual and things secular. Work degenerates to 'tentmaking' whilst we get on with the real work of evangelism.

However, the Bible has a much grander view of the way the people of God relate to the created world. There is no tension between our calling to be witnesses and our calling to exercise rule. Work is not a distraction from doing God's work! Indeed, if we were more effective in our calling to 'rule', we would be far more effective as salt and light in our Christian witness (Matthew 5:13-16).

QUESTIONS FOR DISCUSSION

DISCUSS IT

1. Read Leviticus 19:9-10 and Ruth 2:1-3. What can be gleaned from these passages that is relevant to our own society?

2. Christians are not opposed to some animal rights (see for example Deuteronomy 25:4 and 1 Corinthians 9:7-12). What do we say to people who see no essential difference between the rights of apes and mankind?

3. Does our calling to be salt and light in the world (Matthew 5:13-16) relate to lifestyle as well as to our speaking about the Lord Jesus?

4. We know that remembering the poor is good (Galatians 2:10). Can this be applied to the way companies behave and the way consumers purchase goods?

CHAPTER TWELVE

THE SEVENTH DAY AND THE REST OF GOD

LOOK IT UP

BIBLE READING

Hebrews 4:1-13

INTRODUCTION

It is not unusual for one of my young sons to spend hour after hour working on an invention. This is often a large machine, inspired by tractors working near to where we live, or a combine harvester that we've seen while on holiday. He draws detailed plans of these machines, sometimes identifying the parts. He also draws them working, and demonstrates the extraordinary noises that they make. After all this effort, he takes great pleasure in telling us everything about the machines and how good they are. Sometimes, he ends up physically tired, but this is not normally the case. He rests from inventing machines so that he can show them to us. His enthusiasm for what he has been doing appears to us to be boundless!

Repeatedly in Genesis 1 we read that when God saw what he had made, he declared it to be good. He took pleasure in his creative activity — and it is entirely proper for us to enjoy his creation as well. On the seventh day, when God

For a young boy with plenty of energy, drawing pictures of working machines is a great way to rest!

completed his work, he rested. Of course, he was not tired. He spoke the word, and it was done. These things did not drain him of creative energy. He could make a billion universes and still not exhaust his power.

As indicated above, there are other reasons for resting, apart from weariness. After a painting is created, the artist may rest for a while to appreciate the colours, the composition and the perspectives. There can be great pleasure in resting. A gardener may rest, not because of tiredness, but because of a desire to sit in the garden and enjoy the sight of beautiful flowers, the light and the shadows, and the melodious sounds of songbirds. A teacher may rest from teaching, not because weariness makes it difficult to go on, but because the students need time to absorb and digest what has been taught.

God blessed the seventh day and made it holy (Genesis 2:3). To bless is to bring happiness and satisfaction. The seventh day's rest was a climax and a culmination. Six days were for forming and filling so that the Earth was a fit place for mankind to live. But creating man in the image of God was not an end in itself. God's purpose was not fully achieved by day 6 — more was to be unveiled. By blessing the day and resting, God communicated something very important about his reasons for creating.

Man's task on Earth is to work, to subdue and to exercise dominion (in the Lord's name). But these things are not ends in themselves. There is an ultimate direction for man's life also. Beyond our life's work is a special kind of rest. Beyond tending the garden is entering into God's rest. This is the message behind the fourth commandment (Exodus 20:8-12). God required the Israelites to cease from their labours on the seventh day of each week, because he had rested on the seventh day of Creation Week. The people were to practise the Sabbath Day's rest as a sign of their being in covenant with God (Exodus 31:12-17). The point I am making is that God did not rest just to set a time-table for man. The seventh day's rest goes much deeper than that. His purpose in resting was to point beyond work, towards an eternal rest. It was to stimulate a vision for a deeper dimension to life.

This thought is developed in the New Testament, where we read that the Sabbath was 'a shadow of the things that were to come; the reality, however, is found in Christ' (Colossians 2:17). We truly keep the Sabbath when we rest in him by faith. This is the route to forgiveness of sin, because faith unites us to him in his sacrificial death. This is the route to newness of life, because faith unites us to our risen, triumphant Lord.

PRACTICAL TASKS

How do we enter into God's rest?

Hebrews 4:9-11 says, 'There remains, then, a Sabbath-rest for the people of God… Let us, therefore, make every effort to enter that rest.' We have not understood creation aright unless we understand God's ultimate purpose. If God has set before us in Creation Week the goal of enjoying his rest, how do we enter in to it? Is it not reasonable to think that the whole of Scripture develops this message, and gives us a full answer to this question? Trace God's footsteps through the pages of Hebrews 11 with this question in mind. How do you think the following people might have answered?

- Abel
- Enoch
- Noah
- Abraham
- Moses

Jesus Christ and the rest of God

The Lord Jesus says, 'Come to me, all you who are weary and burdened, and I will give you rest' (Matthew 11:28). The rest that God has planned involves a relationship based on trust and self-giving. The imagery of work is present in the words of Christ: 'Take my yoke upon you... For my yoke is easy...' (vv. 29-30). Man without God is like a fish out of water. Life appears to offer so much, but typically our experience is frustration and dissatisfaction.

King Solomon spent many years searching for satisfaction and meaning from the things this world can offer. He had the riches to seek out all possible ways of reaching his goal, and he had the wisdom to do this well. He was also blessed with the wisdom to assess what realistically could be achieved. His verdict on work is recorded for us in Ecclesiastes 2:17-26. Can man find satisfaction in work? Can he feel a lasting sense of achievement? Without God, the situation is hopeless, for all 'work is pain and grief; even at night his mind does not rest' (v. 23). Only the man who relates his work to 'the hand of God' will escape meaninglessness and find real satisfaction.

Visions of the end

There are a variety of so-called 'scientific' views on the end of everything. You may come across the following three examples.

- *The heat-death view* (unlimited expansion of the universe). The universe appears to be expanding at present and some expect the expansion to continue indefinitely. Stars will burn out, galaxies will die and everything will eventually become as cold as it possibly can be.

- *The big crunch view*. The alternative view is that expansion will come to an end, and the universe will

EXPLANATION

collapse in on itself. Eventually, the whole universe will become a black hole — and who knows what, if anything, will happen then?

- *The reincarnation view* (cyclic universe). This approach postulates a succession of big bangs and big crunches, so that we are said to be part of just one universe out of a sequence of many. This view has a growing number of advocates, because the current 'fashion' in cosmology is to believe in a 'multiverse' rather than a universe. Mathematical models allow innumerable universes to pop into existence and eventually disappear again.

All these accounts take us billions of years into the future (as well as billions of years into the past). There is no acknowledgement that God has brought the universe into existence and that he will bring it to an end at a time of his choosing. These cosmologies have no place for the second coming of Christ and no place for the removal of the Edenic curse in a perfected heaven and earth. The biblical vision of the future is one that involves the transformation of the present order (Revelation 21:4).

Heaven and earth will pass away and there will be 'a new heaven and a new earth' (Revelation 21:1). Death, mourning, crying and pain will be no more (v. 4). In the vision of the new

Jerusalem, the river of the water of life flows from God's throne (Revelation 22:1-2) and on each side of the river is the tree of life, bearing abundant fruit for all who need it. 'No longer will there be any curse' (v. 3). Thus, Eden will be recreated: the river, the tree of life and the removal of the Edenic curse.

Our vision of the end times is inseparable from our vision of the earliest times. If Christians are willing to dissent from cosmological views (on scriptural grounds) when it comes to the end of the age, why do we find it so difficult to do the same when we consider the beginning?

QUESTIONS FOR DISCUSSION

1. *Look again at the 'Three states of creation' illustrated in chapter 6 and read 2 Peter 3:3-13. Why is it necessary for there to be a destruction of the old order and a recreation of heaven and earth? Why cannot the Earth just be cleaned up?*

2. *How do you respond to the Sabbath command? How do you apply the words of Hebrews 4:9-11 to yourself?*

3. *What do you think when you hear scientists speaking earnestly about what will happen to the Earth billions of years in the future? Does the Bible have anything to say about their predictions?*

THE GUIDE

CHAPTER THIRTEEN

THE CASE FOR CREATION (1)

DESIGN IN LIVING THINGS

LOOK IT UP

◀ BIBLE READING ▶

Psalm 139:13-18

INTRODUCTION

Strong witnesses to creation are to be found everywhere. In this chapter, I set out just three evidences, drawn from the world of living things. The basic message I want to communicate is that creation is like an open book. 'How many are your works, O LORD! In wisdom you made them all; the earth is full of your creatures' (Psalm 104:24).

1. The genetic code

Children gain a great deal of pleasure from breaking codes. When a code is solved, an apparently meaningless sequence of letters or numbers turns into a meaningful message. Humans have been very imaginative about coding and decoding techniques. Cracking enemy codes has influenced the outcome of wars. Today, many commercial applications of the Internet are possible only because confidential data can be encoded.

Whether the codes are designed to entertain children or serve the interests of governments, their essential features are the same. Any human code comes with an elaborate coding procedure, a suitable transmission system, and an efficient decoding procedure. The decoded message must be understandable to the recipient — or the whole exercise is a waste of effort.

As soon as it was realized that biological information was transmitted from parents to offspring by means of genes, scientists have wanted to find out the mechanism — how it works. Though the answers are still only partially known, research has uncovered the existence of a code. Scientists refer to it as the *genetic code* and this terminology is highly significant. Some have regarded this discovery as the most important of the twentieth century.

The genetic code is built into the structure of the DNA molecule, which lies at the heart of every living cell. Four different chemical building blocks ('nucleotides') are present. Their function is analogous to the letters of the alphabet. Just as letters are used to construct meaningful sentences, so also are these building blocks used as a template for making the proteins needed by the cell. The nucleotide sequence is a coded message. The message is read and decoded by 'ribosomes', which consist of RNA molecules and enzymes. Their function is to synthesize proteins from amino acids. The outcome is the assembly of the exact proteins specified by the nucleotide sequence.

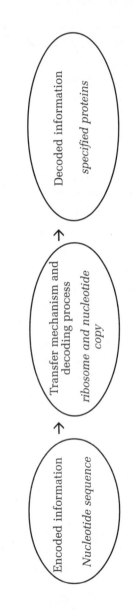

ILLUSTRATION

Encoded information
Nucleotide sequence

→

Transfer mechanism and decoding process
ribosome and nucleotide copy

→

Decoded information
specified proteins

Decoding DNA results in useful biological materials.

The codes we meet most frequently today are computer codes. Intelligent programmers convert real-world problems into a code that is then fed into the computer system. Indeed, both software and hardware are intelligently designed. The analogy with the genetic code is very close — the bio-molecules within the cell are the 'hardware', while the genetic information is the 'software' superimposed upon it.

In our daily lives, whenever we see coding, transmission and decoding taking place, we know that someone has sent a message. Finding a code points clearly to an intelligent agent at work. Codes do not just 'happen'; they have to be designed. One expensive research project is built on this premise — SETI, the Search for ExtraTerrestrial Intelligence. Vast sums of money are being spent, using powerful radio-telescopes to search for signals from intelligent life beyond Earth. How do scientists hope to distinguish intelligent communication from all the radio 'noise' from outer space? By discovering signals containing coded information!

Since, by common consent, coded signals point to intelligence, why should biology be any different? Within every living thing there exists an extraordinarily rich and complex coded system. After much effort by some of the best scientific brains using highly sophisticated technology, we are just beginning to explore the way the genetic code functions. The closer we look, the more pointers we find to intelligent design. For example, the discovery of cases where more than one message is encoded in the same DNA sequence shows

EXPLANATION

that unanticipated sophistication can be found. Other examples are the mechanisms that repair faulty copying. All these data provide powerful evidence that an intelligent Designer has been at work.

No one has yet proposed a coherent explanation of how such a complex coding/transmission/ decoding system could arise by natural processes alone. Nevertheless, evolutionists persist in their view that, one day, an explanation will be found. It is a case of taking an 'evolutionary belief' position contrary to clear scientific evidences of design.

2. The complexity of living systems

When I was a boy, I was able to use a microscope to explore the world around me. It was fascinating to look at printing in books. Under magnification, the letters did not appear crisp and well formed at all! Printed pictures were a chaotic mixture of coloured dots. A razor blade had an edge so jagged that it is amazing it cuts at all. By contrast, living things reveal exquisite details that are unsuspected without magnification. The eye of a fly, the texture of a leaf, the surface of a butterfly wing: these evoke a sense of wonder as we uncover new levels of detail. The contrast with man-made objects can hardly be missed!

The story continues with the help of scientists who have painstakingly explored more and more of these levels of detail. The human body, for example, is an extraordinary system of interdependent parts. Whether we look at the workings of the eye, the ear, the liver, the kidneys or the heart, the closer we look, the more we find systems so complex that they boggle our minds.

Looking deeper still, we find that every living cell is a miniature factory. Each cell has the machinery for carrying out a wide variety of tasks, as well as the ability to replicate itself. The component parts of the cell have all been studied in greater detail, only to find more and more evidence of complexity. We will look at this more closely in chapter 14.

When Darwin proposed his views on origins, the cell was thought to be nothing more than a blob of jelly. It was a simple building block, and there was no reason to think that Darwin's mechanisms for evolutionary change would meet any difficulties changing its form and function. However, as the huge complexity of the living cell emerged, the Darwinian approach appeared less and less convincing. Nevertheless, the theory could be rescued if we were to find simplicity at the most fundamental level of living things.

It was as though biologists are given a Russian doll to examine. Open the case of the outer doll and another is found inside. Split that apart, and yet another pops out. Gradual transformation from simple to complex will always be a problem for evolutionists as long as organisms are found to be sophisticated.

EXPLANATION

Evolutionists need to find the equivalent of a doll that has something inside that will allow their gradualistic mechanisms to work. Molecular biology is recognized widely as the most fundamental level of analysis for any living thing. What will researchers find? Will they uncover at this lowest level some simple system on which Darwinian mechanisms could operate? Or will the final doll of the set be empty, forever blocking Darwinian-type transformation?

Consider the mousetrap, with its base plate, spring, release catch, connector bar and wire hammer. Take away any single element of the mousetrap, and it fails to function. The whole system is designed to catch mice, and even slight changes to the trap can render it useless. Structures like this have been described as 'irreducibly complex'.

In 1996, biochemist Michael Behe published a book with the title *Darwin's Black Box*.[1] He knew that complexity was a threat to Darwinism and wanted to look at the subject more systematically. Behe brought the term 'irreducibly complex' into everyday use, and he popularized the mousetrap analogy above. Behe points out that irreducibly complex biochemical pathways are commonplace — indeed, normal — in living things. He demonstrates forcibly that there is no level of simplicity, wherever we look! Irreducible complexity places severe constraints on the

amount of variation that is possible before the organism ceases to function. If valid, the argument is fatal to
Darwin's theory, which is why evolutionists have
devoted much effort to responding to Behe.

One of the examples Behe uses to demonstrate his
point is with regard to the blood-clotting system. Blood
is an extraordinary liquid. Inside the body, it has to
flow around arteries, veins and capillaries. It gets everywhere, carrying nutrients and oxygen to body cells, and
taking away waste products. However, if the skin is
cut, blood escapes only for a short time. Within min-
utes, a clot forms and the flow from the cut is blocked.
The clot then becomes the focus of healing processes.

Blood contains two proteins: fibrinogen and
thrombin. They are inactive until there is a cut. Then
the thrombin reacts with the fibrinogen to form a clot.
However, there is a problem — the process must be
controlled to prevent clotting throughout the circu-
latory system, which would soon result in death! The
thrombin is therefore stored in an inactive form ('pro-
thrombin'). Clotting then requires an 'activator' to
release the thrombin. This activator is called 'Stuart
factor', which in turn exists in an inactive form that
must first be activated. But Stuart factor on its own
acts too slowly, so another protein ('accelerin') is needed
to speed things up. The story continues with numerous
additional complex proteins and enzymes. According
to Behe: 'The formation, limitation, strengthening, and
removal of a blood clot is an integrated biological
system... The lack of some blood clotting factors, or

EXPLANATION

the production of defective factors, often results in severe health problems or death' (pp. 88-89). Such a system, says Behe, is irreducibly complex and can never have evolved from a simpler form — because that simpler version simply would not have worked!

Darwinism has always claimed to be able to explain the origin of complexity. However, the more scientists look at the data, the less it appears that evolutionary theory has anything helpful to say on this subject. Returning to the Russian doll analogy, the last doll of the set has been opened. It is found to be empty. There is nothing at the core that can be described as simple. Complexity exists in living things wherever we look. Consequently, there is no level at which Darwinian processes of transformation can work. Irreducible complexity is a hallmark of design.

3. Limits to variation

One of the most important biological questions we can ever ask is whether there are limits to variation. Unfortunately, Darwin never asked this question. He appeared to think that all evidence for variation was evidence for his theory. Evolutionists envisage all life to have originated from a single common ancestor. Naturally occurring variations led to speciation and then to more fundamental differences between descendants. This leads to the concept of an evolution-ary tree — a familiar sight in most books about evolu-tion. If all living things today are the result of this process, then there are no significant limits to variation. As we have seen in chapter 9, Bible believers have every reason to question this evolutionary story. In the rest of this section, we revisit the data and its interpretation.

PRACTICAL TASKS

Variations in animals and plants

A significant part of Darwin's *On the Origin of Species* discusses animal and plant breeding. This activity is con-cerned with the results of 'artificial selection'.

If you are a gardener, you are likely to know about new varieties of plants. If you are a livestock farmer, you are likely to know about different breeds of cows, sheep, pigs and hens. Arable farmers will know about varieties of commercial plants. Pet owners may take an interest in different breeds of cats, dogs, pigeons, and so on.

Taking one case known to you, make a list of the vari-ations you can identify. There will be improved traits and weaker traits; there will be characteristics that are present and others that are absent. Consider what happens if these animals or plants are released into the wild.

In the light of what you have noted, are there any pointers as to whether variation can proceed indefinitely or whether it is within limits?

EXPLANATION

It is common knowledge that, by selective breeding, animals and plants can be produced with desired traits (strong muscles, long hair, large fruits and seeds, attractive colours, and so on).

A good example is the domestic dog. Even before it was confirmed by genetics, most people knew that dogs were domesticated from the grey wolf. Whereas wolves have retained their characteristic appearance, the domestic dog is represented by an extraordinary number of breeds. Yet there are limits. By exaggerating certain traits, breeders have created the domestic dogs they want, but these animals are less able to fend for themselves and are more dependent on man. Yet all dog breeds are obviously *dogs*. Breeding has not been able to change their form to such a degree that they cease to be recognized as dogs.

But what about other wild animals that look like dogs? What about the fox, the coyote, the dingo, the African wild dog? Are these linked together by common ancestry like the domestic dog and the grey wolf? To answer this question, we need to look deeper and more systematically. Four lines of evidence are relevant.

a. *Form* (morphology). This is the basic shape and skeletal layout of an animal. It is characteristic for, say, the cat family. All cats,

whether lions, tigers or the domestic cat are, at a
glance, recognizably ... cats!

b. *Cross-breeding* (hybridization data). Cross-breeding
   shows that there is a close relationship between the
   breeding animals. It is not commonly realized that
   hybridization data is available linking many family
   groups of animals and many large groupings of
   plants. Cross-breeding complements the
   embryological data (below) and demonstrates not
   only embryo but also developmental similarities.
c. *Genetics*. Genetic differences can be measured using
   various techniques and this allows scientists to use
   numbers to describe the 'closeness' of these species.
d. *Embryology*. Different types of organisms have very
   different routes of development from single cell to
   foetal animal.

Many dog species can cross-breed. The domestic dog
can breed with the grey wolf, the golden jackal, the
dingo, the coyote, the crab-eating fox, the Bengal fox
and the red fox. Other hybrids are known between wild
species. No crosses are documented between any dog
species and non-dog-like carnivores. Hybrids tell us that
the organisms are linked, ultimately, by common ancestry. Fossil dogs are rare, but recognizable wolf bones
are known from Ice Age sites. There is no gradual transition of fossil forms linking dogs with anything else.

The result of putting all this together is that dog-
like species form a clearly identifiable 'family' distinct
from other groups of animals. It has been described as

EXPLANATION

a 'Basic Type' by Crompton (1993).[2] Variation within the family can be substantial, but there are always boundaries. This picture of 'variation within limits' is found repeatedly in studies of this kind. Such groupings of animals and plants are the norm in nature. Basic Type biology recognizes both continuity (species within the same Basic Type have common ancestors) and discontinuity (different Basic Types have different ancestors).

But is this evidence for creation? Yes, because creation predicts discontinuity between types or 'kinds' of organism. Genesis 1 recounts the separate creation of different types of animals and plants, which thereafter reproduce 'after their kind'. So the original discontinuities are preserved. And that is what we find in nature.

Clearly, the Genesis 'kinds' cannot be linked directly to today's species. In the case of animals at least, the created 'kinds' may be more equivalent to the 'family' level of classification (much bigger than the 'species' level and also broader than the 'genus' level). The dog 'family' is one such example. Whatever the precise nature of the Genesis 'kinds', creation predicts that the living world should look more like a forest than the single 'tree' proposed by evolutionary theory. It should contain many independent trees (kinds), each with its cluster of branches (species). The prediction agrees well with what we find. There is a very good 'fit' between the Genesis kinds concept and the world of biology.

| Elephant Family | Dog Family | Horse Family | Camel Family | Bear Family |

The 'Forest' model of life fits the data well.

QUESTIONS FOR DISCUSSION

1. *The three evidences for creation outlined in this chapter can be considered to be the tip of an iceberg. Different issues make different impacts with different people, so your personal 'three evidences' may not be the same as mine. What are your three best evidences for creation (in the living world)? How do you explain these evidences to others?*

2. *Have you experienced a part of your own body malfunctioning? If so, did you discover more about how it is supposed to function normally? Did the experience*

DISCUSS IT

teach you anything about the complexity of the human body? Does this knowledge affect the way you think about origins?

3. *In February 2003, the finding of a new species of plant in northern England was declared to be a triumph for Darwinism. 'Darwin was right and the creationists are wrong!' wrote the reporter.*[3] *The new species was a hybrid of two wild species of groundsel. Does this new species really support Darwinism? How would you explain the significance of the discovery to someone?*

4. *Read God's words to Job (chapters 38-41) with the thought that creation is like an open book. Why is it that none of Job's friends helped him to read this book?*

THE GUIDE

CHAPTER FOURTEEN

THE CASE FOR CREATION (2)

DESIGN IN THE NON-LIVING WORLD

LOOK IT
UP

BIBLE READING⟩

Psalm 19:1-6

INTRODUCTION

In the previous chapter we looked at three evidences for creation drawn from our knowledge of living things. Just as the living world bears witness to God's handiwork, so also does the non-living world. 'The heavens declare the glory of God; the skies proclaim the work of his hands. Day after day they pour forth speech' (Psalm 19:1-2). In this chapter we consider three further lines of evidence, all of which show design in the non-living creation. In each case, scientists are amazed at the 'fit' between the inanimate world and its ability to support and nurture life.

1. The uniqueness of Earth as a 'prepared planet'

As we have noted in chapter 7, the Earth is a planet formed by God to support life. It was prepared for life. With a generation of space probes behind us, it has become obvious that the Earth is unique in our solar system in that it is eminently suitable for life.

*Earthrise, as seen by the Apollo 8 astronauts
as they orbited the Moon, 21 December 1968.*

(Courtesy of NASA)

One of the most evocative images of the Earth is one taken from the Moon. In the foreground is the baking hot, airless lunar surface. In the distance is a blue planet with white clouds, wonderful because it has an oxygenated atmosphere, comfortable temperatures and water in abundance. There's nothing like planet Earth! The reason for this is given in Genesis 1. It is different because it was specially prepared for life.

WORK AT IT

PRACTICAL TASKS

Select a children's book on astronomy that deals with our planetary system. List all the planets and draw up a table of comparisons. Factors you ought to include are: surface temperature, atmospheric pressure, presence of oxygen, presence of water, gravity, and distance from the sun.

- What life support systems are needed on each planet?
- How does the Earth compare with the rest?
- Is it correct to say it is unique?

(If you want to extend this activity, include the major moons in the solar system alongside the planets.)

However, some insist the Earth is not unique. They argue that there are millions of planets out there like ours. Such thinking typically underplays those features of Earth that can be understood as having been designed. There are over 100 known planets outside our solar system, but none of them give any encouragement for thinking that Earth-like planets are numerous. If we look for a scientific assessment of the situation, we must conclude that the Earth is unusual. This message is conveyed in the title of a recent book on the subject, *Rare Earth*.[1]

2. The design of the elements to support life

Have you ever thought how unusual liquid water is? When it freezes, a large amount of heat energy is given up. When it becomes a gas, an even larger amount of heat energy is absorbed. These properties are unusual, but without them, the Earth's surface would experience extreme fluctuations in temperature. Water at 4°C is heavier than ice. This means water freezes at the top of ponds, lakes and seas. Living things in the water are protected by the ice, and not killed by it. Furthermore, water is a remarkable solvent, indispensable for the working of cells and so essential for life. No other liquid can match its properties. Rarely do we reflect on how distinctive these characteristics are.

There are explanations, of course, coming from science. A molecule of water is made up of two hydrogen atoms and one oxygen atom. The distinctive properties of the hydrogen and oxygen atoms are crucial to scientific reasoning. However, it is often the case that textbooks report the facts but fail to infer design in both water and its building blocks.

Hydrogen and oxygen do not just combine to form water. They are present in most biological materials, often combining with other elements like calcium, sodium, potassium, iron, and so on. Many biological structures and processes are built around the distinctive chemical and physical properties of these elements. Sodium, potassium and chlorine are highly reactive

EXPLANATION

elements, but when they have reacted, they form very stable compounds. Consequently, they have a very important role in maintaining the stability of fluids, whether inorganic (the oceans) or organic (body fluids, blood). They maintain fluid concentrations and osmotic balance. Calcium and magnesium form some readily soluble compounds (so they can be transported in rivers and body fluids) and also some hard insoluble compounds (so they can be used to make shells, bones and teeth). Simply to study them is enough to stretch the mind and to leave us amazed at the intricacy of it all.

We must ask the same question as before. Are these remarkable structures and processes a coincidence, with 'natural selection' making the best use of available resources, or are these things designed? It is not unusual for scientists to use phrases like 'marvellous' and 'exquisite' in their descriptions of structures. How much more should Christians give glory to God! (Psalm 104:24; 139:14).

3. The 'fine tuning' of fundamental constants

Cosmologists have developed mathematical tools in order to explain how the universe works. Most cosmologists start off with the idea that our universe is nothing special and that the values of the constants they use in their equations are accidental. However, these values have proved to be anything but accidental. Their precise values can make all the difference between success or failure of the models.

As an example, take the strong nuclear force that is responsible for binding together protons and neutrons in the atomic nucleus. If the force is too weak, the models predict that the universe would be dominated by hydrogen for ever (because the nuclei of all other elements would be unstable). If the force is too strong, the models predict that all the hydrogen would become helium and heavier elements; in which case, there would be no water and no life. According to the models, the chemistry of life is very sensitive to the value of the strong nuclear force. The scientists involved have been left wondering whether the value of this force is a happy coincidence or whether it has been determined by a wise Creator.

Over the past twenty years, it has been found that all cosmological models are tightly constrained by the values of these fundamental constants. The constants are not arbitrary. They are highly specified, and this has led to their being described as 'fine tuned'.

The UK Astronomer Royal was so impressed by this finding that he wrote a book about it in 1999, entitled *Just six numbers*.[2]

These six numbers constitute a 'recipe' for a universe. Moreover, the outcome is sensitive to their values: if any one of them were to be 'untuned', there would be no stars and no life.

It has not escaped the attention of cosmologists that if these constants do not have arbitrary values, then it is a fair inference that they are designed. This, for example, comes from the journal *Nature*, 14 November 1996:

> It turns out that the physical constants have just the values required to ensure that the Universe contains stars with planets capable of supporting intelligent life...The simplest interpretation is that the Universe was designed by a creator who intended that intelligent life should evolve. This interpretation lies outside science.[3]

The idea that science can provide evidence of a creator/cosmic intelligence is alarming to many scientists. The major response to date is to speculate about innumerable parallel universes, all different and with different fundamental constants, with ours just having the right values to support life. Thus, our universe only appears to us to be unusual — in the parallel universes model it is just as arbitrary as the rest. This idea was greeted initially as absurd, but it has now reached the status of being the majority view.

EXPLANATION

According to the Astronomer Royal:

Is this tuning just a brute fact, a coincidence? Or is it the providence of a benign Creator? I take the view that it is neither. An infinity of other universes may well exist where the numbers are different. Most would be stillborn or sterile. We could only have emerged (and therefore we naturally now find ourselves) in a universe with the right combination.[4]

This appeal by scientists to an infinity of undetectable, unprovable parallel universes might seem paradoxical, but it is what happens when people with a mindset that has no place for God come face to face with evidences for creation. Instead of acknowledging design and the necessity of a Creator, these scholars will dream up ways of evading the conclusion, even if this takes them down the pathway of fantasy.

Conclusions

This chapter commenced with some words from Psalm 19 on the way the inanimate creation provides a rich testimony to the glory and wisdom of God. This witness can be appreciated at every level — through the eyes of a child or through the studies of experienced scientists. Let us revel in it and give God the honour! We should rejoice in the works of his hands!

CONCLUSIONS

Someone suffering from blindness cannot appreciate the way the Earth is filled with light, colour and visual beauty. Someone suffering from deafness lives in a world where spoken communication and music is a mystery. Our hearts go out to these people because of their handicaps. In this and the previous chapters, we have looked at some very broad and wide-ranging evidences for creation. These evidences are not hidden to our generation, because they are introduced in schools and they crop up repeatedly in the media. Why are they not recognized as evidences for creation?

In some cases, there is no response because people are blind or deaf to the evidences. They have no sensitivity to these issues. In other cases, extraordinary avenues of thought are devised to escape the design inference. What about you? Are you aware that you are surrounded by abundant evidences of God's design and his creative work? Does your heart go out to those who live as though they are blind and deaf? How do we help those who live as though God is irrelevant to the universe, the Earth and human beings?

QUESTIONS FOR DISCUSSION

1. *The apostle Paul wrote that people will deny that God's eternal power and divine nature can be*

clearly seen (Romans 1:18-20). What is it that can be clearly seen?

2. Should we be witnessing to people about creation? Is it better to be witnesses to Jesus Christ and leave belief in creation until after people have come to faith? Can we be faithful witnesses to Jesus Christ without addressing the issue of creation?

3. Science fiction may bring the excitement of exploring worlds beyond our own and of encountering extra-terrestrial beings. However, does this literature have other, less desirable, effects upon us?

4. God's world is noiseless, low energy, economical, self-balancing and self-cleansing. If we see ourselves as ruling the world around us, should we be patterning our stewardship on God's example? Make a shortlist of priorities for change.

CHAPTER FIFTEEN

THE CASE AGAINST EVOLUTION

BIBLE READING

Romans 1:18-20

INTRODUCTION

A century after Darwin, a landmark book was about to be published with the title, *Implications of evolution*. The author, Professor Kerkut, recounted his experience of interviewing biology students. He would ask them about the evidences for evolution, and they usually offered something in response. Then he would ask them about the evidences against the theory. This was invariably met with blank expressions and some would blurt out, 'But sir, there isn't any!' Even after they had time to research the issue, they could not identify scientific arguments against Darwinism. That, said the professor, flags up a problem. Students were not developing critical faculties but soaking up standardized answers. This was not, and is not, a healthy situation for science.

If we want to think clearly about these issues, we must distinguish between historical science and empirical science. Empirical science majors on laboratory experiments, under the control of the researcher. It seeks to advance our understanding of the physical world through cleverly designed experiments that give repeatable results. Historical science, on the other hand, considers non-repeatable past events, deals with circumstantial evidence, and seeks to identify unique causes.

In some disciplines, it is acceptable for scientists to infer the past activity of intelligent beings. For example, forensic science seeks to identify human agents who commit crimes. Again, archaeologists aim to distinguish natural objects from artefacts crafted by man. The actions of intelligent beings can be handled within science — so this is not where controversy lies.

Evolutionists, however, allow only natural causes in their approach to origins. This means that intelligent causation by God is ruled out as an option. Using this methodology, no 'reputable' or 'competent' researcher is allowed to arrive at the conclusion that an intelligent Creator has caused anything. At best, there may be a Creator who establishes the laws of nature and chooses to operate only through natural processes.

The case against evolution, then, must take the form of a 'trial by jury'. The prosecution has to demonstrate that the theory fails to achieve an explanation of origins by means of natural causes. It must show that there is a mismatch between evolutionary theory and science, in that its predictions fail (or that it distorts the evidence to make it fit). The case against evolution, if it is to be successful, must reveal genuine gaps in the chain of natural causes — these gaps are the telltale signs of inadequate explanations.

PRACTICAL TASKS

It is useful to check the relevance of the material in this guide by doing a small survey of your own. Find ten people who accept an evolution- ary explanation of origins. They do not have to be scientists, but if they have a scientific back- ground that is a bonus. Ask them to respond to these questions:

1. What are the main reasons why you accept the theory of evolution (three reasons will suffice)?
2. What evidences are you aware of that are against the theory of evolution?
3. Has your acceptance of evolution influenced your thinking about God?

Questions 1 & 2 will help you to appreciate the material in this chapter. Question 3 will help with assessing the relevance of the guide as a whole.

1. The origin of life is a complete mystery

In Darwin's day, there was considerable open- ness to the idea that God created the first living cells. Thereafter, many claimed, Darwinistic mechanisms came into operation and the process of evolution led to all the living forms we see today. However, all the modern textbooks of evolutionary theory have a section dealing with the origin of life without involving God. All these books suggest that life originated in the Earth's distant past through unguided natural processes. Students are left in no doubt that life emerged in the distant past when 'the conditions were right'.

Nearly always, the starting point is the 1950s research of Stanley Miller. He made a mixture of hydrogen, water, methane and ammonia (to mimic a hypothetical early-Earth atmosphere); simulated lightning using electrical discharges; and devised a way to accumulate reaction products. From these simple gases, Miller found he could make amino acids, the basic building blocks of life. These were supposed to have accumulated in pools or lakes on the primeval Earth, forming an environment (the so-called 'primeval soup') that allowed the first living cell to emerge.

Within a decade, serious objections were raised. The 'atmosphere' used by Miller was unrealistic because it had too much hydrogen and not enough carbon dioxide and oxygen. When a modified atmosphere of nitrogen, carbon dioxide and water (still no oxygen) was used, the yield of amino acids was nil. If oxygen is added to any mixture of gases, it is even harder to produce amino acids.

The Earth's early atmosphere should have left some pointers to its composition in the 'basement' rocks. A lively debate has taken place over the past fifty years, with some claiming evidence to support Miller's 'atmosphere'. However, the majority view is that these

EXPLANATION

evidences are either misread or point to local conditions that were not representative of the Earth as a whole. Geologically, a strong case can be made that there has always been oxygen in the Earth's atmosphere. If oxygen was present, amino acids could not have been formed. However, such was the impact of Miller's experiments that the issue continues to be raised again and again. Evolutionists 'know' that Miller's atmosphere 'must have existed', because otherwise they cannot explain the origin of life! So they keep on looking for it.

But even if they are right, it does not help them. The accumulation of amino acids would not bring about the origin of life. When Humpty Dumpty fell off the wall and broke into pieces, all the king's horses and all the king's men could not put Humpty together again. It is just the same with living things. Everyone knows that if we take living cells and fragment them, they will not reassemble. Even if we mix all the necessary molecular 'building blocks' together to form a 'soup', life does not emerge. Furthermore, amino acids are the most basic components of cells, and some of the other ingredients are far more difficult to form. For decades, clever scientists, using the most favourable conditions, have played around trying to make a self-assembling living cell. They have failed totally.

So difficult is the task that many scholars are looking for other ways to assemble life. Some

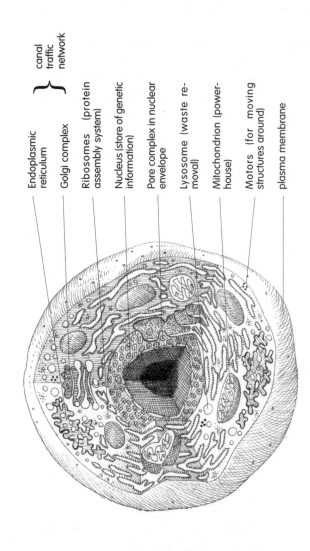

Endoplasmic reticulum

Golgi complex

} canal traffic network

Ribosomes (protein assembly system)

Nucleus (store of genetic information)

Pore complex in nuclear envelope

Lysosome (waste removal)

Mitochondrion (powerhouse)

Motors (for moving structures around)

plasma membrane

The animal cell is a miniature factory full of micro-machines in a state of continuous activity. It used to be thought of as a blob of jelly!

favour an oceanic ridge environment, where molten rock interacts with sea water. Some favour the Earth's crust, where complex chemicals have a chance to exist for longer because oxygen cannot get at them. Some look for cells to form in the atmosphere. Some feel the task is hopeless, and that the Earth must have been seeded with life from Mars or from outer space. Each year brings new ideas, but the quest for a convincing solution goes on!

The more we know about living things, the more we discover the complexity of the cell. It is not a simple blob of jelly but a miniature factory full of micro-machines and packed with biological information. A factory may have automated assembly machinery within it, but it does not self-assemble. This is also true of the cell. The idea that living things emerged from non-living chemicals is devoid of any scientific support, either in theory or practice. The myth should not be perpetuated in textbooks. To the question, 'Can life arise spontaneously from non-living matter?', scientific research gives a clear answer — a resounding 'No!'

2. Darwinian mechanisms are inadequate

Before Darwin, no one had come up with anything capable of producing major transformations —

but Darwin created the impression that his theory was workable. He had two mechanisms: variation and natural selection. Did they work? There has been near continuous controversy over this within the academic world. It is by no means universally accepted that these mechanisms can deliver the transformations Darwin claimed.

Some of the variation Darwin discussed can now be discounted. All organisms have genetic mechanisms ensuring that offspring differ in many small ways from their parents. But Gregor Mendel, working with sweet peas, demonstrated that all the variations he observed come from genetic information that was *already present* in the plants. Such information can never change one kind of organism into another. This was a blow to Darwinists, but they bounced back by introducing mutations — random changes in the genetic material that arise from various causes (e. g. radiation or chemical damage). Mutations might, in principle, create novel variations because they alter the genetic code. So Darwinism became neo-Darwinism and claimed to be fully compatible with the science of genetics.

Unfortunately for this theory, however, nearly all mutations turn out to be damaging. For example, the list of mutations known to affect humans continues to grow, but these 'variations' are *never* welcomed as contributing to human evolution. Quite the contrary; doctors hail 'gene therapy' as a new way to treat genetic accidents (mutations) that invariably cause disease. The failure of Darwinists to give good examples of *beneficial* mutations is highly significant. The proposed mechanism for creating new biological infor-mation appears instead to have a consistent tendency towards degeneration (as is illustrated by the oft-quoted cases of bacterial resistance to antibiotics and sickle cell anaemia).

Natural selection is the other key mechanism identified by Darwin. However, selection forces have proved to be so weak that they are very dif-ficult to study in the field. Very little progress was made for about 100 years. Then in 1959, an article appeared in the journal *Scientific Ameri-can* with the title 'Darwin's missing evidence'. This was Bernard Kettlewell's work on 'evo-lutionary' changes observed in populations of light and dark coloured peppered moths. After another fifty years, Kettlewell's triumphant claim is an embarrassment. His experiments were poorly designed because when he released the moths, they settled on tree trunks, where birds could find and eat them. However, in the wild, these moths only rarely settle on tree trunks. The photographs shown in textbooks are contrived, the moths often being glued in place. In reality, the experi-ments reveal how complicated natural selection is. (Incidentally, the peppered moths remained peppered moths; no genuine 'evolution' occur-red, even if Kettlewell's results were valid.)

The other major example of natural selection in action relates to the finches of the Galapagos Islands. There is no doubt that selection effects are present, but no one knows whether the observed variations involve any genetic novelty. The variations relate to body size and beak dimensions, and the changes are reversible. There is nothing that can be extrapolated to achieve the transformations that Darwinism claims to explain.

Natural selection appears to be a weak force in nature. It helps to maintain the health of a population, and it allows some adaptation to changing environmental conditions. However, its ability to transform a population of organisms into something new has never been demonstrated. Nevertheless, Darwinists cannot discard this mechanism. Their problem is that nothing else has been proposed that can do any better.

The combined mechanism of 'mutations + natural selection' has become a magic wand. Wave it — and dinosaurs grow feathers and fly; fish grow legs and walk; apes get clever and become human. It is amazing what can be achieved with a lively imagination — but even more amazing how little actual evidence there is to support the theory!

Before the period known as the Scientific Revolution, alchemists were inspired by the grand vision of transforming base metals into gold. Their labours paved the way for the science of chemistry, but their ambitions got in the way of the science. Today, Darwinists are the alchemists of biology. Their transformist agenda gets in the way of genuine science. Like the alchemists of old, there is a complete mismatch between their mechanisms for transformation and the real world.

3. The fossil evidence for large-scale transformation is negative

EXPLANATION

Evolutionists have always considered that the fossil record provides evidence for their theory. However, a closer look reveals that all is not well with their arguments.

Darwin made an important prediction in the *Origin of Species*, and it caused him some difficulty. His mechanism of evolution was linked to small variations and required gradual change. The prediction was that although gradual transformation is hardly noticeable over our timescales, it would be apparent over geological timescales. However, his gradualistic prediction is not what is observed. Hence, to preserve his theory, Darwin had to claim that the fossil record is imperfect.

Over a hundred years passed, and the scientists who study fossils kept searching for better sequences that would show transformation. They found an odd-looking bird with some reptilian features, but nevertheless this was a true bird with feathers for flying. They found an assortment of fossil horses that were put together artificially to show increasing size and changes to toes and teeth. However, these so-called 'successes' actually show that there are enormous problems in documenting gradual transformation. This is not at all what the fossils reveal!

The record of hard-bodied fossils has a remarkable beginning. Representatives of most of the animal groups (identified by body plans) are found typically at the same horizon in the rock record. This has been termed the 'Cambrian Explosion'. It is notably non-Darwinian, because so much novelty occurs in a very small interval of geological time. One of the best ways to appreciate this point is to look at the fossil record of trilobites. These marine animals appear suddenly in the fossil record, and they are far from simple. They have a segmented body, most have complex eyes and their development involves shedding their exoskeleton as they grow in size.

In the 1960s, a radical break with Darwin's prediction took place. It came about because scientists could not accept that the fossil record was so imperfect. They found the same patterns over and over again. They noted that fossil species appear abruptly in the fossil record, continue with minor changes (stasis) and then become extinct. 'Stasis is data', they argued. The new approach soon became dominant, because stasis is what the scientists actually find. Evolutionary ideas are still held, but there has been a shift away from Darwinian gradualism. However, there is a theoretical vacuum, and we still await a coherent statement of what the new evolutionary theory is. While this situation exists, Darwinism reigns in the textbooks and among most evolutionary biologists.

In summary, Darwin predicted an evolutionary tree. This was the one illustration he included in the *Origin of Species.* The fossil record does not supply it. The data shows a forest (see chapter 13). Evolutionary transformations are usually represented by dotted connecting lines bridging the 'gaps' between fossil species — the data is lacking.

Concluding comments

These examples have shown that evolutionary theory fails the science test. The gaps are real and the data points away from the evolutionist predictions. However, evolutionists cannot escape from their predicament unless they shift their position and allow into their science the possibility of there being an intelligent cause.

It has often been said that 'more research' will solve the mysteries: 'Science will find the answers.' Part of the case against evolution is that this has led to closed minds. Science starts with the quest for knowledge and the excitement of discovery. It teaches students to have open minds, a questioning approach, and a willingness to challenge ideas that are inadequately tested. However, the dead hand of evolutionary theory has now created a generation of people who are mentally numb. The research reviewed in this chapter has shown that the likelihood of finding natural explanations for life's origins has diminished steadily as research has progressed.

The recognition of design is a legitimate part of science. The challenge for scientists today is to grapple with the claim that living things carry the hallmarks of design. Once this is regarded as a legitimate issue for scientists to discuss, there will once again be an openness to knowledge — wherever it may lead. When this happens, it will point to an improvement in the health of the scientific community.

QUESTIONS FOR DISCUSSION

1. *Why is it that so few are aware of any evidences against evolution? If you were one of Professor Kerkut's students, how would you answer his question on page 196?*

2. *Students are repeatedly told that only the theory of evolution allows us to make sense of biology. Is this really the case? Is there anything else that allows us to make sense of biology?*

3. *The common examples given of evolution in action today (melanism in peppered moths, Galapagos finch beaks) reveal only variation within the Basic Type (see chapter 13). What kind of evidence is needed to support the main claims of Darwin's theory? Do we have it?*

4. *If it is the case that 'gradual transformation' is largely absent from the fossil record, why is it widely regarded as giving support to Darwin's theory?*

READ FURTHER

For further reading

More thorough treatments of the issues covered in this chapter are found in the following sources.

Kerkut, G. A. *Implications of evolution*, Pergamon Press, London, 1960.

Kettlewell, H. B. D. 'Darwin's missing evidence', *Scientific American,* vol. 200 (March), 1959, 48-53.

Wells, Jonathan. *Icons of Evolution*, Regnery Publishing Inc., Washington, 2000.

See also: www.biblicalcreation.org.uk/introductory-articles/bcs084.html

AFTERWORD:
CHRIST IN
CREATION

CHRIST IN CREATION

I can remember looking at the Moon in 1969, thinking how extraordinary it was that two men were walking, at that very moment, on its surface for the first time. News reports said that the first man on the Moon was Neil Armstrong. However, anyone looking for photographic evidence to prove the statement will have to report failure. All the astronaut images relating to the first lunar landing are of Buzz Aldrin. Yet, this lack of photographic evidence does not affect the historical record. We have other evidences, including the testimony of reliable witnesses, that Armstrong was first. In recent times, there has been an upsurge of Moon-landing deniers, who claim that the lunar landings were faked by NASA. The whole exercise, these people say, was a contribution to the cold war between the United States of America and the Soviet Union.

Yet what would we say to someone who claimed that the facts are of no importance? What would we think of the argument that historical accuracy does not matter because the story is inspiring? Someone might say: 'The imaginary stories show that the spirit of mankind can reach beyond the confines of the Earth.' I do not think we would be impressed by this thought. The significance of any human achievement cannot be based on idealism. There must be a foundation in history. The facts *do* matter! Without such a basis, we might as well spend our time dreaming about what life could be like or indulging in science fiction.

History matters!

But what about going further back in history? What about events in the lifetime of Jesus Christ? We have the testimony of faithful witnesses that he performed miracles of many kinds. Hundreds witnessed the reality of his resurrection from the dead. The disciples thought that the physical resurrection was vital to their message. Nevertheless, others have claimed that the history is not important. Those taking this view have turned the gospel message into a dramatic fictional story that inspires the human spirit. However, Christians rightly reject this approach. Unless Christ really is raised from the dead, our faith is in vain (1 Corinthians 15:14). Facts *do* matter!

But let us go back further. What about Moses? Was he a real person? Was he used by God to lead the Israelites out of Egypt, turning them from slaves to free people? And was Abraham a real person? Did he leave Ur at God's command and did he father Isaac in his old age? Going back still further, did Noah really build an ark? Did God really bring the animals to the ark so that they could be saved while the rest of the world perished? Did the people before the Flood live for about 900 years? Does it matter if this part of Scripture is invented? Are these early chapters concerned with real events and real people?

This guide has examined the first four chapters of Genesis, with Adam and Eve, Cain and Abel, and their immediate descendants. We have looked at the Scriptures and found them to be historical in character. Repeatedly, we have found that the New Testament writers make a link between historical reality and meaning. Those who want to find meaning in the words whilst abandoning the history are failing to think biblically.

In this guide, we have avoided the use of the term 'literal'. For some, it is the hallmark of faithfulness. For others, it means being simplistic, wooden, and insensitive to the cultural context. My own view is that the term is not helpful for clarifying the issues. The New Testament puts the emphasis on the historical realities of the people and events of which it speaks, and that is the emphasis we should be following.

The meaning of creation history

We have reviewed the role of Christ in creation. He was God's agent of creation. Through him all things were made. We have seen Christ as God's agent of providence. Through him, God upholds all things that he has made. Paul writes of 'The Father, from whom all things came and for whom we live; and there is but one Lord, Jesus Christ, through whom all things came and through whom we live' (1 Corinthians 8:6). Father and Son are co-workers in creation and in providence. Without this emphasis our theology is deficient.

We have considered many different teachings that are grounded in the early chapters of Genesis. We neglect these chapters to our loss, for we shall lose touch with many foundational themes of the Christian faith. Most importantly, we lose the context for presenting the gospel, for man's true condition (rebellious and disobedient, alienated from God and under judgement) can only be understood properly from the vantage point of Genesis 1 - 4. This is why the issue of origins is central for Christians: the message of the gospel is affected if we move away from biblical teachings about who we are, who God is and how we have come to be in need of salvation.

Christian scholarship

Christians are concerned with truth. God's revelation in nature is not in conflict with his revelation in Scripture. We are called to use our minds and to engage with evidences. Ultimately, our attitude towards science is positive. We delight to study God's world and we admire his handiwork! We need to use our minds to ask the right questions and to seek out satisfying answers. We have considered some aspects of this in more detail in chapters 13 and 14.

The providence of God is foundational to science (as we have seen in chapter 2). In the same way, the knowledge that man is made in the image of God is foundational to the disciplines of history, linguistics, politics, art, sociology and psychology. Without it, scholars are like people who sail in ships without rudders or anchors. Such people drift before winds and currents without the control provided by a rudder and without the security provided by an anchor. Young people studying at school or at university need to have this wisdom of God so that they can relate their studies to God's revelation. Failure in this area has been a disaster-zone for Christians. Young people are often woefully unprepared to engage with the world of scholarship.

Creation is a key part of God's revelation to us: we keep coming back to it. We must not let ourselves be robbed of God's truth because we are intimidated by the 'wisdom of this world'. We need a generation of Christians who understand the times in which we live and can apply God's Word to the issues of our day. The academic community today exists in a spiritual vacuum. Revelation has been rejected as a source of knowledge, so we are left with a power struggle between naturalistic science ('nature is all there is') and post-modernism (relativism and 'our world is socially constructed'). As Christians, we have all we need to fill this vacuum with true knowledge. The foundations are in Genesis 1 - 4.

The goal

If we are to be biblical in our understanding of creation, we must recognize that Jesus Christ is the central figure. Not only is he the agent of creation and the upholder of all that has been made, but he is also the goal of creation. He is the theme of the Sabbath-rest. My prayer, as author, is that you are blessed in reading *The Guide* and involving yourself in the activities and questions. My concern is that Christians come confidently to these parts of God's Word and fearlessly apply the truth of God to the issues of our day. But we only truly believe in creation when we have entered into God's rest by faith in Jesus Christ. So my prayer also is that we are diligent to enter that rest (Hebrews 4:11). The promise of God is sure. We are invited to come boldly before his throne, that we may obtain mercy and find grace to help in time of need (Hebrews 4:16).

THE GUIDE

NOTES

NOTES

Chapter 1: Understanding Genesis

1. H. Schulz, *Old Testament Theology*, Vol.1, p.25.
2. P. J. Wiseman, *New discoveries in Babylonia about Genesis*, Marshall Morgan and Scott Ltd, London, p.101.
3. *Ibid.*, pp.148-9.
4. *Ibid.*, p.147.

Chapter 4: Humanity bears the image of God

1. Roger Highfield, 'Do our genes reveal the hand of God?' *Daily Telegraph*, 20/03/2003.

Chapter 13: Design in living things

1. Michael J. Behe, *Darwin's Black Box*, The Free Press, New York, 1996.
2. Source material for 17 Basic Types (animals and plants) is in *Typen des Lebens*, Pascal-Verlag, Berlin, 1993. The dog family is identified as one of the Genesis kinds by Nigel Crompton: 'A review of selected features of the family Canidae with reference to its fundamental taxonomic status', pp.217-24.
3. Report on the new species in *The Times*, February 2003.

Chapter 14: Design in the non-living world

1. Peter D. Ward, Donald Brownlee, *Rare Earth,* Springen-Verlag, New York Inc., 2000.
2. Sir Martin Rees, the Astronomer Royal, *Just six numbers*, Weidenfeld & Nicolson, London, 1999, p.4.
3. 'On the likelihood of habitable worlds', *Nature*, J. M. Smith & E. Szathmary, 14 November 1996, p.107.
4. Rees, *Just six numbers*, p.4.

For a more detailed treatment of some of the evidences presented in this chapter, see *Mere Creation*, edited by William Dembski, IVP, 1998. Also 'Designer Earth' by Arthur Jones, available on the Biblical Creation Society web site at www.biblicalcreation.org.uk.

THE GUIDE

RECOMMENDED FURTHER READING

The literature on creation and origins grows significantly every year. The titles below offer a range of follow-on reading on subjects addressed in this guide.

Andrews, E. H. *From nothing to nature*, Evangelical Press, Darlington, 1978.

Andrews, E. H. *Christ and the Cosmos*, Evangelical Press, Darlington, 1986.

Baker, S. *Bone of contention*, 3rd edition, Biblical Creation Society, Rugby, 2003.

Blanchard, J. *Evolution – fact or fiction?* Evangelical Press, Darlington, 2002.

Burgess, S. *He made the stars also*, Day One Publications, Epsom, 2001.

Burgess, S. *Hallmarks of design*, 2nd edition, Day One Publications, Epsom, 2002.

Currid, J. D. *Genesis*, Volume 1 (1:1 - 25:18), Evangelical Press, 2003.

Johnson, P. E. *Darwin on trial*, 2nd edition, IVP, Illinois, 1993.

Johnson, P. E. *Testing Darwinism*, IVP, Leicester, 1997.

Kelly, D. F. *Creation and change*, Christian Focus Publications, Ross-shire, 1997.

Peet, J. H. J. *In the beginning God created…*, Grace Publications Trust, London, 1994.

A wide range of excellent books on spiritual subjects is available from Evangelical Press. Please write to us for your free catalogue or contact us by e-mail.

Evangelical Press
Faverdale North Industrial Estate, Darlington, DL3 0PH, England

Evangelical Press USA
P. O. Box 825, Webster, New York 14580, USA

e-mail: sales@evangelicalpress.org
web: www.evangelicalpress.org